SWING LIKE A PRO

SWING
Like a
PRO

THE BREAKTHROUGH METHOD
OF PERFECTING YOUR GOLF SWING

DR. RALPH MANN

and

FRED GRIFFIN

with Guy Yocom

Broadway Books   New York

BROADWAY

Broadway Books titles may be purchased for business or promotional use or for special sales. For information, please write to: Special Markets Department, Bantam Doubleday Dell Publishing Group, Inc., 1540 Broadway, New York, NY 10036.

BROADWAY BOOKS and its logo, a letter B bisected on the diagonal, are trademarks of Broadway Books, a division of Bantam Doubleday Dell Publishing Group, Inc.

Library of Congress Cataloging-in-Publication Data
Mann, Ralph, 1949–
    Swing like a pro : the breakthrough method of perfecting your golf swing / by Ralph Mann and Fred Griffin with Guy Yocom. — 1st ed.
      p.   cm.
    Includes index.
    ISBN 0-7679-0236-X (hc)
    1. Swing (Golf)   I. Griffin, Fred, 1956– . II. Title.
  GV979.S9M25   1998
  796.352′3—dc21
                                                      98-23534
                                                       CIP

FIRST EDITION

Designed by Sam Potts
Cover photos by Lee McDonald
Photography by Jim Moriarty

20 19 18 17 16 15 14 13 12

Contents

Acknowledgments

Supporting Staff

We would like to give special thanks to Phil Rodgers, Chuck Cook, and the late Davis Love Jr. for their inspiration and support in our efforts to understand the great game of golf.

Thanks also to the core group of teaching professionals that have helped us understand how to apply this information to our students. They include Lee Houtteman, Todd Meena, Kevin McKinney, Eric Eshleman, Joey Hidock, Gary Smith, Lars Hagglund, Carl Alexander, Harry Zimmerman, Adrian Stills, and Gus Holbrook. Added thanks to Doug Lowen, whose ability to mimic the swing errors common to all golfers was essential to this effort.

Without the behind-the-scenes efforts of the researchers, this work would be little more than educated guesswork. They include Curtis Cowan, Jimmy Vespe, Sid Sachs, Ron Linares, Bob Hilts, Amber Murphy, John Kotmel, John Herman, Charles Fisher, Charlie Schultz, and Paul Sprague.

Finally, we thank our wives, Angela and Jackie, for their encouragement and understanding that our passion for studying the game always took more time than we estimated.

Players

We want to thank the following tour players for volunteering their swings for our research efforts. A model swing is only as good as its components, and we think this group is tough to beat.

Tommy Aaron	Brandel Chamblee	Ray Floyd
Kristi Albers	Bobby Clampett	David Frost
Helen Alfredsson	Keith Clearwater	Jim Furyk
Fulton Allem	Dawn Coe-Jones	Buddy Gardner
Buddy Allen	Charles Coody	Jane Geddes
Donna Andrews	John Cook	Al Geiberger
Stuart Appleby	Ben Crenshaw	Gail Graham
Wally Armstrong	Joe Daley	Lou Graham
Paul Azinger	Bruce Devlin	Hubert Green
Seve Ballesteros	Dana Dormann	Tammie Green
Chip Beck	Bob Eastwood	Gary Hallberg
Woody Blackburn	Danny Edwards	Phil Hancock
Brandie Burton	Bob Estes	Morris Hatalsky
Joanne Carner	Brad Faxon	Mark Hayes

Vance Heafner   Barb Mucha   J. C. Snead
Tim Herron   Jodie Mudd   Ed Sneed
Lon Hinkle   Bob Murphy   Mic Soli
Scott Hoch   Jack Nicklaus   Craig Stadler
Mike Hulbert   Greg Norman   Sherri Steinhauer
Hale Irwin   David Ogrin   Payne Stewart
Betsy King   Mark O'Meara   Dave Stockton
Tom Kite   Arnold Palmer   Mike Sullivan
Gary Koch   Jesper Parnevik   Bob Toski
Ralph Landrum   Mark Pfeil   Ted Tryba
Bernhard Langer   Don Pooley   Kris Tschetter
Franklin Langham   Dicky Pride   Bob Tway
Bob Lohr   Tom Purtzer   Tommy Valentine
Davis Love III   Nancy Ramsbottom   Lanny Wadkins
Scott McCarron   Loren Roberts   Grant Waite
Gary McCord   Hugh Royer   Duffy Waldorf
John Mahaffey   Charlie Rymcr   Colleen Walker
Meg Mallon   Nancy Scranton   Lisa Walters
Roger Maltbie   Scott Simpson   Dennis Watson
Doug Martin   Tim Simpson   D. A. Weibring
Len Mattiace   Val Skinner   Jay Williamson

Foreword

All golfers want to improve their game. Whether your goal is to win a major tour event, improve your chances at the club championship, beat the members of your foursome, or simply break 100 for the first time, the desire to improve is universal. The appeal of golf is partly due to the fact that everyone, regardless of ability, can experience a longer drive, straighter short iron, and more accurate short game. And until someone shoots a 50, there is always room for improvement.

Tour players, like everyone else, are continually looking for an edge. Because the difference in being on top of the money list and failing to retain your playing card can be as little as one stroke per round, it is easy to understand our desire to excel. So, we find the best equipment, practice long hours, and find the best instructors to help us improve our swings.

All of this effort can be ineffective, or even detrimental, if the information we receive is even slightly flawed. Valuable practice time is wasted. The more effort you pour into perfecting the swing, the worse you can actually become. Frustration mounts. Since our livelihood is at stake, needless to say we strive to obtain the best information possible.

This desire for solid information on the swing was the main reason I was attracted to the work being done by Ralph and Fred. It is comforting to know that my swing is being compared to the best swings over the past twenty years, and the goal is to improve even more on the swing components that have made these players successful.

Understanding what to improve is the key to getting better. In my case, it was encouraging to know that my swing already contained most of the correct fundamental movements. That gave me confidence, and as all golfers know, confidence in your swing is just as important as dedication on the practice tee.

I have known Fred for many years and as a result, I have sought his advice on helping me improve my full swing technique. Once you see the model and study it closely, both your weaknesses and strengths become easy to identify.

The information contained in this book can be used to both identify and improve your golf swing. And as you begin swinging more like the Pro, you'll also develop the confidence that comes through knowing that your swing is moving closer and closer to the swing we would all like to have.

Brad Faxon

Introduction

Golf is a very difficult game.

And yet, when watching a great pro swing the motion seems so smooth, so fluid, so natural. It looks simple. But as the millions of amateur golfers who strive to develop a proficient swing can attest, it is more difficult than it looks.

The golf swing is not simple. It is enormously complex, perhaps the most challenging sport we humans do for recreation. Errors of a small fraction of an inch or a minute change of angle lead to large differences in the direction and trajectory of the shot, and where the ball comes to rest.

Unraveling such complexity in a movement that occurs so quickly requires rigorous observation and research. This book reports the results of fundamental scientific research, and its application, that Dr.

Ralph Mann and Fred Griffin have been conducting over the past seventeen years on the mechanics of the golf swing and improvement of amateur golfers.

Having the right information is essential to executing a good swing—one that controls where the ball goes and is consistent and reproducible time and time again. The research they have conducted has given us this information.

But helping you to become a better golfer requires more than good information. Early in the research process, they both recognized the need to be able to communicate this information to students in such a way that permanent improvement is the result. Their experience has given us valuable insight into the most productive way to apply their findings to all levels of golfers.

In short, they have methodically determined both what to teach and how to teach the golf swing. And their conclusion is that permanent improvement, as distinguished from the quick fix that doesn't last, will result from understanding the golf swing: understanding what must be done to strike the ball well, how your swing compares to a great swing, and how to make your swing better.

Within this introduction, Dr. Mann offers insight from a scientist's viewpoint, while Fred Griffin discusses a teacher's outlook on this innovative learning process.

THE SCIENTIST

by Ralph Mann, Ph.D.

I am a scientist. Scientists work by making objective measurements of the phenomena they are studying and then developing a theory or model that predicts behavior. For the past seventeen years, my colleagues and I have used scientific methods to study the best golfers in the world. Many have been to our laboratory: Jack Nicklaus, Greg Norman, Davis Love III, Tom Kite, Brad Faxon, and Ben Crenshaw, among others. This book tells you what we have found and gives you a way to use this information to improve your performance and deepen your understanding of the golf swing.

The purpose of this book is to make you a better golfer. The bookshelves are full of these types of books, but you will find this one radically different. The difference is that we deal in fact, not opinion. We face reality, not fantasy.

The truth is that there are many inherent problems in the game of golf, as well as in the way it is taught. These difficulties can be summarized as follows:

- Golf is a stagnant sport—the quality of play has not improved the way it has in many other sports during the past thirty years.
- While other sports have embraced well-defined paths for long-term improvement, a similar system has yet to be discovered in golf.
- Golf instruction tends to be based on individual opinion rather than fact-based research.
- Golf instructors tend to be excellent teachers, but the information they provide to students is often seriously flawed.
- There is a widespread yet mistaken belief that a good golf swing can be done numerous ways.
- Golfers have erroneously been convinced that there is one key to a better golf game.
- Golfers have been indoctrinated with the erroneous belief that if one player does something unconventional, it's OK for everyone.
- Instructors and sports psychologists frequently promote the belief that your swing can get better without changing your swing.
- Equipment manufacturers have oversold the notion that golfers can buy a better game.

If these statements pique your interest, read on. If you are ready to embark on a path that will let you understand both *the* golf swing and *your* golf swing, then forge ahead. If you are tired of quick fixes and would rather opt for long-term improvement, this book is for you. Golf is too great a game for you to waste your time on things that have limited the sport for so long.

THE EVOLUTION

There have been two personal characteristics that have shaped everything I have done in my life. Ever since I can remember, I always asked questions. It is inherent in my nature to attempt to understand everything around me, much to the consternation of my friends and family. This trait caused me to gravitate toward the area of science, which is populated with people like myself.

The second trait has always been my ability to run fast. As a child I ran everywhere I wanted to go, and even today I derive great enjoyment from that activity. The fact that I was always faster than most of my peers naturally enhanced my love for the sport.

As I got older, these two seemingly unrelated skills dramatically affected my life. Since my science interests were always application oriented, I studied engineering in college. My running became more serious as I quickly discovered that although I wasn't fast enough to win any world-class sprint races, I could use my height as an advantage in the hurdle race.

As you would expect from a scientist, I set out to be the most technically proficient hurdler who ever competed. I obtained films of the best hurdlers, then used my engineering skills to analyze and mimic the best in the world. My talents and persistence took me a long way. I was the slowest sprinter in the finals of the 1972 Olympic 400-meter hurdles, but my technique enabled me to finish second (fig. I-1). It is ironic that the winner, who broke the world record by almost half a second, had absolutely no interest in technique. He just ran then jumped when the hurdles got in the way.

My two loves, science and athletics, came together when I visited a sports research lab in East Germany. I was introduced to biomechanics, the science of us-

FIG. I-1. Since I didn't have the natural speed necessary to contend at the world-class level, I had to rely on technique to be competitive.

ing engineering techniques to study human motion. It was a match I couldn't resist. So I went back home and obtained my doctorate in that area. The advent of computers provided the opportunity to analyze human motion in much greater depth. My required dissertation was on computer modeling, where I took the best athletic performances and combined them into a single superior movement.

When I began teaching at the university level, I also began analyzing elite athletes in a wide variety of sports. Since that time I have been fortunate to analyze and work with some of the best athletes in Olympic track and field, Major League Baseball, all three of the major professional golf tours, the National Football League, and several of the minor Olympic sports. Of all these sports, golf has been both the most interesting and the most unusual.

I've been analyzing golf for almost seventeen years, and there is no other sport quite like it. My extensive background in other sports, my observation of the game from both the outside and the inside, and my research orientation, combined with the fact that golf was not my chosen sport, has allowed me to make conclusions about the game that contrast significantly with beliefs that have been accepted in the teaching community for many years.

GOLF: THE STAGNANT SPORT

As all sports progress, they evolve from part-time players participating for enjoyment to full-time athletes getting paid handsomely for their efforts. As the stakes increase, the rewards attract better athletes who seek innovative ways to enhance their performance. Top athletes in many sports have their own coaches, psychologists, nutritionists, biomechanists, and physiologists. Many of the more technical sports have groups of scientists and coaches who specialize in the science of the sport. The most startling example was the success of the East German sports science effort in the 1970s and 1980s, the fruits of which revolutionized sports as we know it.

The Germans were so successful that the Americans were forced to turn to sports science in order to remain competitive. Since that time, I have seen the performances in the international sports improve dramatically. The swim times of the Olympic champion Johnny Weissmuller would not qualify him for most good high school swim teams today. Jessie Owens's sprint times of the 1930s would be insufficient to earn him even a chance at qualifying for a contemporary Olympic team. In virtually every advanced sport, the athletes of yesterday would have no competitive chance against the athletes of today.

In golf, the story is much different. Much has been made of the statistic that handicaps have not improved for the average golfer over the past twenty years. But it's a potentially misleading statistic due to the changes in the type of people who play golf now as opposed to the past. If you want to use comparisons to determine the advance of the sport, look at the performances of the PGA Tour players of today with those of the past. Sadly, despite significant advances in equipment design, improved course conditioning, and much greater prize money, tour players of today perform little better than their counterparts of twenty years ago.

There are numerous reasons for this stagnation; however, the primary problems stem from four diverse areas: elitism, money, complexity, and teaching.

Elitism

Due to the nature of the game, golf has been and will probably continue to be a sport for the privileged. Although past restrictions related to social standing are disappearing, the inherent barriers of taking up the game will always be present. I lost the Olympic gold medal to an athlete from Uganda who was from a poor family of more than thirty children. The only equipment John Aki-Bua required were his shoes, and some sticks to jump over. Golf, which requires expensive equipment, some formal training, and extensive travel in the formative stages of a player's career, will never generate this type of story.

Money

In professional sports, the athletes follow the money. In professional baseball, a good utility infielder can make more than the leading money winner on the PGA Tour—and the baseball player's salary is guaranteed! From this standpoint, golf has always been at a severe disadvantage. Golf has been blessed with some fine athletes, including such stars as Greg Norman and Nick Faldo. It has not, however, seen the equivalent of a Michael Jordan or a Wayne Gretzky. Tiger Woods may fill this role; however, the monetary incentives to produce several of these types of athletes are missing in golf.

Complexity

Golf is an intricate game, in many areas. Phil Rodgers once commented that there have been less than a hundred players who have really played the game. To master all aspects of golf, from the full swing to the short game, and understand how to put it together on the course, is a monumental task. The sheer complexity serves as a barrier that steers many athletes toward other sports.

Teaching

To put it bluntly, virtually every popular golf teaching system is opinion based. Nothing is wrong with innovative opinion challenging the status quo of the sport—most innovation occurs in this form. Unfortunately, there have been no unassailable criteria by which to determine correct from incorrect. So golfers who seek the answer in books and magazines continue to run around in circles, trying the latest "magic move" that probably was presented to their fathers twenty years earlier.

In 1972, track and field was, like golf, dominated by opinion-based coaching information. Since that time researchers have eliminated those opinions that were faulty and begun to focus on fact-based research findings. Thus, the circular trap of pitting one opinion against another was broken, and the sport was empowered to move forward.

Golf, unfortunately, remains on the circular path, with one opinion accepted with as much credibility as another. Despite well-intentioned efforts to provide credible paths to learning, information today is no better than it was twenty years ago.

The inherent problems of elitism, money, complexity, and teaching have severely limited golf development. I can't do anything about the first three problems. I can, however, address the teaching issue. After years spent researching and applying the information in a controlled teaching environment, our results can be used to dispel the erroneous beliefs and support the correct observations.

GOLF INSTRUCTION— HOW TO TEACH AND WHAT TO TEACH

After observing the world of golf instruction for almost seventeen years, I have arrived at a couple of conclusions. First, having observed teachers and coaches in many elite sports, golf instructors rank, hands down, at the top of the list of those who know how to teach. I have observed some of the best instructors in the game, and have been greatly impressed with the talents of instructors such as Bob Toski and Jim Flick and their ability to communicate. This capacity to work with people falls in the category of "how to teach," an area in which golf instructors excel.

Second, there is the matter of "what to teach." In this area, golf unfortunately falls at the very bottom of the list of the elite sports I have observed. There is so much contradictory opinion on golf instruction that most teachers are overwhelmed by the challenge of determining what to teach.

Several teachers have impressed me with their ability to wade through all of the contradictory information and come up with answers that are close to being on the mark. Ben Hogan was probably the most technically astute observer of the game, although his personality did not lend itself well to teaching. David Leadbetter and Hank Haney are modern-day examples of instructors who have done an excellent job of discerning what to teach.

Davis Love Jr. and Phil Rodgers are examples of instructors gifted in both of these areas. The fact that the personalities of both of these men were different, both emotionally and communicatively, indicates that sound, diverse teachers can come from any direction.

As a scientist, I am concerned with the what-to-teach aspect of golf instruction. Given good information, the sport will progress. Given the talent and dedication of golf teaching professionals, the sport will surely make great progress as more good information becomes available. This is the contribution science can make to the sport.

GOLF INFORMATION—OPINIONS VS. FACTS

Information used in golf instruction has been opinion dominated for so long that both teachers and golfers, more often than not, assume that these opinions are somehow based on factual information. The opinion of a successful instructor or player may be accurate, useful, and valuable; however, it should be regarded as exactly what it is—an opinion.

Science is very specific and deals only in measurable, quantifiable facts. By examining these facts and determining explanations for why they are so, scientists make theories that explain behavior. The role of the scientist in sports, therefore, is to determine facts that point to the key features that makes a successful performance.

Opinions and Pseudoscience
Opinion-based instruction articles are fine. Many of the most innovative approaches in teaching have come from such sources. A major problem arises, however, when such articles purport to be "research based." I have a folder full of articles that make conclusions on the golf swing that are "based on ten years of research" which, under close examination, translates to "I videotaped a lot of swings and I've looked real closely at them for a long time." In the world of scientific publications, any research information is closely scrutinized by other scientists before it can be accepted for publication in any professional journal. This guarantees the quality of the information and protects the

credibility of the scientific profession. Currently, no such checks are in place in the golf publishing community, and the term "research" can be utilized without any kind of scrutiny.

For any profession to achieve credibility, its research must be monitored and above reproach. When opinion is presented as research, people have no way of determining what is good and what is bad in the area. Unfortunately, this is the state in which golf instruction currently finds itself.

Research

By accepted scientific standards, relatively little proper research has been done on the golf swing. There have been a few interesting publications, such as *The Search for the Perfect Swing* by Alastair Cochran and John Stobbs, and a few conferences on the science of golf; however, little of this information has been related to the human component of the golf swing. Our research on the full swing seems to be unique, which is unfortunate because the best science results when researchers confirm and build on the work of each other.

Sports research seeks to understand the movement elite athletes make in producing a superior performance. Defining that movement in mathematical terms of space and time is the problem to be solved. The solution process lies in making precise measurements—ones that cannot be tainted by individual opinions and prejudices. The final result will determine the common features that are essential for superior performance.

The scientific research process is complicated by the fact that individual skeletal and muscle structures are not the same, which affects how people move and how their bodies perform. So these variables also need to be studied using the same rigorous measurement and analysis methods. Despite these physical differences among people, it may surprise you that we, as well as other sports researchers, have found an astounding similarity in how the better athletes perform in every sport analyzed. Despite the complexity of the human body, the evidence is overwhelming that there is one best way to perform any given sports activity.

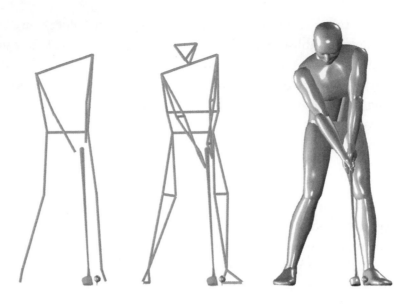

FIG. I-2. Over time the sophistication of our research information, as well as how we represent the model swing, has evolved considerably. The figure described with lines has been termed "stick man" while we have named the 3-dimensional image "the Pro."

THE BIOMECHANICS APPROACH— THE MODEL SWING

Whether the sport was track and field, tennis, baseball, or football, by combining biomechanics and statistics, we have been able to determine a list of things that elite athletes do to ensure a superior performance. The most surprising thing is the long length of the list and how far above the average athlete the elite performers operate. For each of these sports, we have combined these elite movements into what we call a model performance.

Golf is no different. In 1982 we began filming tour players, and to date, the list has grown to include over one hundred PGA, LPGA, and Senior PGA Tour players. Along with the increase in the number and quality of our athletes came a similar improvement in the sophistication of our analysis and our ability to represent the model. Over the years we have progressed from a stick-figure representation to three-dimensional models of world-class male and female golfers (fig. I-2).

The "model" swing concept does not lack controversy. I constantly hear the comment from golf instructors that since all golf swings are so different, there is no such thing as a model swing. Rather than try to convince them with research and statistics, I simply ask them if they teach every one of their students to stand on both legs to hit the golf ball. Since they all do, I point out that they have just described the beginning of their concept of a model golf swing. I quickly get them to agree on other components, such as using both arms, holding the club with the hands, and placing the ball on the ground. They laugh and tell me that these things are obvious—it's the complex parts of the swing that are different.

In any aspect of life, things become complex when you encounter the unknown. Knowledge allows the complex to become simple. That certainly is true in golf instruction; the more you know about the golf swing, the easier it gets—provided your information is correct.

Building a True Model

The model golf swing, like all other sport models we have developed, is much more than simple averages of the elite athletes. A true model identifies the best characteristics of the entire group of athletes, then channels all of these traits into one performance. Thus, both our men's and women's tour model not only has the best strength, flexibility, and body build to play the game, but also all of the movement patterns required to hit the ball long and straight (fig. I-3).

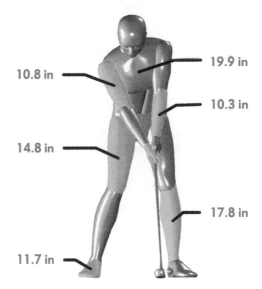

FIG. I-3. The model swing has the best characteristics of the greatest tour players in the game. Not only does he have the perfect build for golf, but the perfect balance of strength, flexibility, and coordination. All of these traits allow him to produce the swing that has the strengths of all the players, rolled into one.

Individualizing the Model Swing

When we first began applying our research information to teaching, an obvious problem manifested right away—most people aren't built like the typical tour pro. In fact, we noticed considerable adaptations even in the professional swings due not only to body height and width, but to seemingly minor differences such as arm and leg length, the ratio between the length of the upper and lower body, and shoulder and hip width. While we were able to eliminate these differences during our analysis, we were now faced with the problem of reinstating them so we could use the model information to instruct people of all body types (fig. I-4).

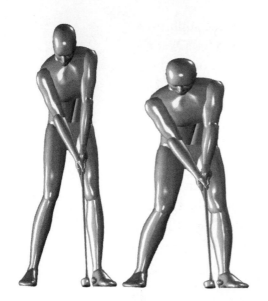

FIG. I-4. The challenge was to be able to adjust the model swing to fit the body dimensions and club selection of any size student and still retain the characteristics of a model swing. There are obvious setup differences between a tall, thin golfer (left) and a short, broad golfer (right), but the critical setup positions are identical.

The ability we developed to adjust for body type not only allows us to use the model to teach any individual, but also provides great insight into the way swings change due to the wide variety of human beings we encounter in the teaching process. It is comforting to know that, although many subtle alterations are made in the swing due to the difference in body build, there still remains an extensive list of movements that must be produced if a quality golf swing is to be created.

Exceptions

Whenever I present our research results in golf, someone will invariably disagree with at least one of my points and offer, as proof, some well-known professional whose swing is at odds with my findings. What many people don't understand is that research is not concerned with the exception, but rather the typical. Our goal is to find out what the majority are doing because that's where the true success story lies.

If one hundred of the best players in the world align their 3-irons down the target line at the top of the swing, and Jack Nicklaus aims his 30 degrees across the line, this position is probably not one of Jack's strengths. In fact, much of what he does in his swing is done to minimize his tendency to hook the ball from this position.

Applying the Model Swing

Over the past seventeen years, we have been using the model to help instructors in their effort to teach the golf swing. In turn, the experience has given us numerous new avenues of research opportunities and a better understanding of the game.

THE MYTHS OF GOLF

Golf is replete with myths—stories that are widely believed but are not based in proven fact. There are myths about how to swing, myths about equipment, myths about how to improve. Our research enables us to shed light on some of these myths.

Swing Myths

This book describes what needs to be done to develop a proficient swing. There are several popular ideas, however, that need to be avoided by those hoping to improve. The following are commonly held beliefs that I find insupportable by the information gathered in our research on the golf swing.

1. One Move to Better Golf

Any number of people claim to have discovered the "one move to better golf." The fact that so many have been proposed is a strong indication that none really exists. The one move that Greg Norman needs to use to keep from pushing the ball to the right under pressure and the one move that Tom Lehman needs to avoid pull-hooking the ball under the same circumstances have no relation to each other.

As much as we would like it to exist, there is simply no one move that will make everyone a successful golfer. If you want to improve your game, you have to understand the causes for your particular problem, then take the time to correct them.

2. All Swings Are Different

There are many ways to swing a golf club—that's why we keep handicaps. Our research has indicated, however, that there is one best way to get the most from the body and club movements. The swings of lower-handicap players come close to matching this model swing; tour players come the closest.

All golf swings can be placed in two categories: people who slice the ball and people who hook the ball. Those who are in the middle are simply being successful at avoiding one of these categories. Our experience has been that approximately 90 percent of developing golfers either fade or slice the ball. This is true because virtually all of the errors that are made in the golf swing result in either a more vertical or a more outside-to-inside swing path on the downswing.

On the other hand, if you overdo most of the beneficial moves in the golf swing, you will produce draws or hooks. Experience tells us that while poor players constantly slice, the better players constantly fight a hook.

3. Arms Lead the Swing

Some instructors firmly believe that the arms lead the swing, and the body follows. In absolute terms, there is no sport that involves striking or throwing an object in which the arms lead the action. Those teachers who profess that the arms lead the golf swing are doing their students a grave disservice. In fact, the higher the handicap of a golfer, the more the arms tend to lead the swing since poor golfers don't involve the lower body. In contrast, the more proficient the golfer, the more the body leads the swing—with the arms and club following.

4. Swing Plane

The term "swing plane" is one of the most often used buzzwords in golf. It is visualized as a flat surface that the club swings on throughout the entire golf swing motion. In fact, there is no such plane in the golf swing. A proficient golf swing begins on one plane and continually shifts throughout the swing (fig. I-5). Our instructors use the term "swing path." This is done since a path can twist and turn as it moves, whereas a plane must follow a flat surface. The mere use of the term "swing plane" helps to create a mental picture of a swing that is incorrect.

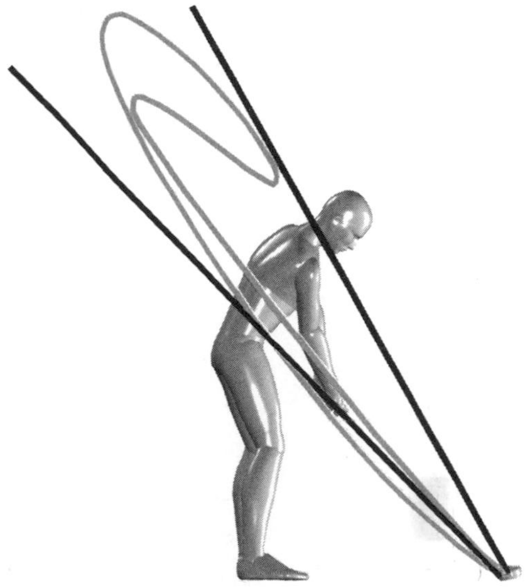

FIG. I-5. Regardless of where you place the swing plane (black), it doesn't match the actual path of the clubhead (blue) on either the backswing or the downswing.

5. Stay Connected

There is a school of thought that contends the arms should stay "connected" to the body during the swing. This improper action is the major cause of slicing—perhaps more than any other single misconception. In fact, the arms must move independently of the body if they are to produce the correct swing path.

6. Swing in a Barrel

It is the belief of several golf instructors that the swing should be able to occur as a totally rotary movement. They emphasize that the swing should be envisioned as a turning effort in a barrel. In reality, there is no throwing or striking activity that does not involve moving the body laterally to produce the required power. If you look at power players such as Hogan, Norman, and Woods, you see enormous lateral movement. In our teaching, we do see golfers who succeed in "turning in a barrel"; however, they have difficulty breaking 120 on the golf course.

Sports Psychology Myths

The current vogue in golf is to improve your game through positive thinking. It is very enticing to think that a simple good thought and positive attitude will improve your swing.

This type of errant psychology is what I term the "I believe in myself" approach. When sports psychology was first applied to Olympic athletes, a large number of the psychologists were using this approach. It didn't take long for the athletes to realize that just thinking you can do it simply didn't work very well when the competition actually began.

The psychology concept that has found lasting success focuses upon the concept of "I understand myself." This approach teaches athletes to understand both their strengths and their weaknesses so they can work within their capabilities. If the best drive you ever hit went 230 yards in the air and the carry over the water in front of you is 229 yards, you are probably not going to reach dry land. The "I understand" group will help you recognize that, due to your limitations, the potential success of that shot probably isn't worth the penalty failure will exact. Therefore, hit the drive to the safe landing area, and accept the fact that you probably will only par the hole. Accept the fact, that is, until you can get to the practice area and continue working on increasing your distance off the tee.

The second type of psychologist is the one whom we employ in our programs. They may not be as flamboyant, and they may not sell as many books, but in the long run they are much more effective.

Equipment Myths

I wish I could say that money can't buy a better game. In truth, golf equipment has evolved to the point that it can make a difference. The same player using a $3,000 set of clubs will play better than if he is hitting a $300 set. Equipment matters, but there are limitations. The right club will moderate your slice or give you five more yards more off the tee, and the result is that your scores will improve slightly at the outset. Yet there is an illusion there, because equipment will not erase flaws in your swing. Eventually, poor technique will come back to haunt you. So buy the best equipment you can afford, but understand that the true road to improvement is in developing a better swing.

The Myth of Hope

Everyone wants to hit the ball like Greg Norman. Greg has great talent, is a fine athlete, and works on keeping fit. Most of all, he spends countless hours on the practice tee. The bottom line is this: if you want to get better, you must invest serious time in your game.

On the other hand, dedication alone may not be sufficient. We had a prospective PGA Tour player move to Orlando, where he proceeded to spend ten hours a day for an entire year working on his game. He didn't ask for help since he knew what he wanted to work on. We just watched him, day after day, work on a series of bizarre swing motions. After a year, his actual swing looked like his practice swing, and he couldn't break 85. Dedication is required, yet watching this fellow hammer away unproductively proved you must also be set on the proper path.

THE CHALLENGE

For all the approaches used to improve performance, one bottom-line strategy is guaranteed to make you a better player. That strategy is to improve your full swing. Hitting the ball straighter and farther with more consistency is the one surefire route to improvement. That's what this book is about.

All of the information that follows is based on sound, proven research. Every critical position and movement has been found to be a significant factor in producing a great golf swing. And as my partner, Fred Griffin, will discuss, it has been presented to give you not only the knowledge but also a way to make the model swing a part of your game.

I hope you relish the information presented in this book as much as I have enjoyed the research process required to obtain it.

FIG. I-6. The goal of a teacher is to success-fully communicate good information to his stu-dent, then help him to design and execute a plan to improve.

THE TEACHER

by Fred Griffin

I am a teacher. Golf teachers want to improve their students by giving them the ability to hit good shots consistently. To do this a teacher needs good information, a clear understanding of what needs to be achieved, and a plan to get there that is consistent with the student's ability and commitment to improve (fig. I-6).

My experience indicates that at least 90 percent of those who read this book will have the same goals: to become more consistent, elimi-nate a fade or slice, and hit the ball farther. These goals can be achieved for most people, but doing so will not be easy. You will first need to understand the information presented in this book. Unfortunately, understanding alone will not retrain your body; that will take time and effort. The information provided herein has the potential to lead to dramatic improvement, but only after a long period of retraining and many hours on the practice range.

THE EVOLUTION

Of the many sports I have played since I was a child, golf has captivated me most. I vividly remember, at age twelve, our family moving into a new house directly across the street from the eighth hole at our local country club. I'm not sure who was more excited, me or my parents. Me, for the fact that I could ride my bicycle to the course whenever I wanted, or my parents because I would stop hounding them constantly to drive me to the course. Even then I knew somehow that golf would be at the center of my life.

I experienced reasonable success as a junior, amateur, and college golfer, though not so great as to convince me to try seriously to play the PGA Tour. In 1980, a family friend told me about a course that Jack Nicklaus was building just outside Austin, where he was going to be the director of golf. He mentioned that a position would be available in the golf department. I took him up on the offer. A unique feature of this project was an Academy of Golf, a dedicated practice facility with three practice holes designed to teach golf to players of all skill levels. As part of my duties, I was to spend part of my time working at the Academy.

The director was a teacher by the name of Chuck Cook, who was a regular instructor for the *Golf Digest* schools before joining the Academy. Several weeks before the Academy was scheduled to open, Chuck organized some training classes to familiarize the staff with the teaching philosophies that would be utilized. After attending these training sessions, I knew that teaching golf was what I wanted to do for my career. Fortunately, Chuck recognized my interest to become a teacher and hired me to work full time.

While working at the Academy, I had the opportunity to observe some of the top teachers in the golf industry, including Davis Love Jr., Dick Aultman, Paul Runyan, Jackson Bradley, Harvey Penick, and Phil Rodgers. Being exposed to these teachers enabled me to learn a tremendous amount of information about the game and influenced many of the teaching ideas that I use today.

I was particularly impressed with Phil Rodgers's understanding of the swing, and how easily he could improve a student's ball flight (fig. I-7). He really understood the cause-and-effect implications of the swing and could instantly detect the most important change that needed to be made. He also was and is renowned for his short-game ability, which I witnessed many times. Phil would say that you are not always going to hit perfect shots, but you can make up for the ones you miss with a good short game. He taught his students to never give up on a hole, even after a couple of bad shots because you might hole a 30-footer to save your score.

FIG. I-7. Phil Rodgers is recognized as one of the best and innovative teachers in the game of golf.

Along with bringing top teachers to the Academy, Chuck would invite specialists in the field of sports science. We conducted a school at the Academy with Dr. Ralph Mann, a biomechanics expert, in which he filmed each student's swing and then compared them to a model he had developed from filming some of the best swings on the PGA Tour. I was impressed with his scientific approach and the ability to discover and explain the student's specific swing flaws utilizing computer technology. I realized that this type of technology would be the next step in golf instruction, and I wanted to be a part of it.

In 1985 I took advantage of a great opportunity and became the director of golf at The Grand Cypress Academy of Golf in Orlando. During our first year of operation, Phil and I made a proposal to the owners of Grand Cypress to include Dr. Mann's technology as part of our program. One of my goals as director was to establish a teaching program at the Academy that was based on fact, not opinion. Dr. Mann's research-based teaching would enable us to provide consistent instruction throughout our teaching staff. One of the main complaints I hear from students over and over is that they are told one thing from one instructor and something entirely different from the next. This is an ongoing problem in golf instruction, and I am sure it will continue so long as the information being taught is based on opinion.

THE MODEL

Dr. Mann's introduction details the modeling process that he developed to produce the model swing. I witnessed this research process and can testify that it is extremely rigorous (fig. I-8). To analyze one swing on the computer takes approximately two full days. The film speed runs at 500 frames per second, and the entire golf swing takes just under two seconds to perform. Therefore, to gather information on one swing from two views, the technician needs to analyze 2,000 frames of film. To make matters even more difficult, the technician must follow only one point on the body at any one time. For example, from the face-on view he would follow the right elbow throughout the entire swing, then he would rewind the film and follow the right wrist, right shoulder, and so on. In all, the technician follows thirty-one points on the body, and five different points on the club, totaling 72,000 pieces of information on one swing. To analyze over a hundred PGA and LPGA Tour players, each taking up to six swings with different clubs, was a mind-boggling task.

Dr. Mann's model reflects the best elements of the swings of some of the best players ever to play the game. The model also focuses on the strengths of these elite players and eliminates the weaknesses that

FIG. I-8. The first step in the analysis process is to collect high-speed film of the tour player hitting a wide variety of clubs.

they all have. The end result is a swing that will be consistent in producing the best combination of power and accuracy.

When I am asked to present the information on the model to teaching professionals or tour professionals, someone will always make the point that everyone swings differently and that there is no such thing as an ideal swing. I believe, however, that all good teachers have a generalized model swing in mind that they try to teach to their students. Furthermore, the better the teacher, the more specific the model. They will be very precise with how the body, arms, and club should function during the swing.

THE TEACHING LABORATORY

We have utilized this model information and applied it to golfers of all ability levels for the last eleven years (fig. I-9). Over this period, we

Before   After

FIG. I-9. Technology has allowed us to show the student his swing, with his own model superimposed. This ability to visually show the student what is needed to improve has made the teaching process much simpler.

have given over 40,000 individual lessons using the computer technology developed by Dr. Mann.

Once you have developed a standard to measure by, and then compare it with the swings of thousands of golfers of varying ability levels and body sizes, certain swing tendencies that are commonly repeated can be easily identified. For example, the number-one trend demonstrated by novice golfers is the tendency to position the ball too far back in the stance at address. This is done because they do not utilize the entire body during the swing and, therefore, they release the club prematurely and strike the ground toward their back foot. I could easily list seven or eight more trends that are constantly demonstrated by students attending our golf schools.

One of the most significant things I have learned from working with the model swing is that the body controls the club. Many times we as teachers or students are constantly working on getting the club into a correct position at some point in the swing, when we should really be focusing on the body. For example, during the takeaway, when the club is at hip level and horizontal to the ground, most instructors want to see the club parallel to the target line. As a result, almost all golfers make the mistake of taking the club too far to the inside at the beginning of the swing. This is caused because they overturn their hips early in the backswing. If the hip turn is reduced, the position of the club will improve immediately. My point is, it is the body that puts the club in a poor position—or a good one.

Working with such a large number of golfers has also given us insight as to how best to teach the swing. In order of priority, I focus on correcting the lower body first, then move to the upper body, and finally work on the arms and the club. Many times if you get the first two right the last two will fall into place.

CONSISTENCY AND THE GOLF SWING

One of the questions we ask our students is their improvement goal for their teaching session. The number-one answer, hands down, is that they would like to become more consistent in their ball-striking ability. They recognize they have the capability to hit good shots, but they simply don't hit them often enough.

After the first day of instruction, it is easy to identify the faulty swing mechanics limiting their consistency. The most obvious problem is failure to set up the ball correctly at address. And the reason for that is they are compensating for the flaws that they consistently produce in their swing.

That's right. All golfers produce the same errors in their swing, time and time again. Many golfers think that when they hit a good shot they have produced a good swing, a swing entirely different from the one that sliced the ball out-of-bounds to the right. Not so. When Dr. Mann and I began applying the model in teaching situations, we had the students select the swing that produced their best shot for comparison with their model. We found their best swing was no different from their worst swing, regardless of the quality of ball flight.

Good shots result from poor swings on occasion because of last-instant manipulation of the club that successfully squares the clubface at impact. The problem is, these compensating manipulations are impossible to perform precisely every time. The poorer the swing mechanics, the more compensations that need to be made and the more inconsistent the shots.

Yes, you do have a repeating swing—one that produces inconsistent shot patterns. To become more consistent, you need to improve your mechanics. You need to swing more like the model.

Even with a proficient swing, you will still miss many shots during a round of golf. The goal is to make those missed shots more playable and less penalizing. Even the great Ben Hogan stated that in a round of golf, he would hit only a handful of what he considered good shots. But the ones that were not as good were still playable ("eminently serviceable," he said) and allowed him to save his score. That is our goal in working with students. The way to become a more consistent ball striker is first to identify what your poor tendencies are and then work to reduce them as much as you are physically able. By so doing I promise that your improved swing will produce more good shots and, ultimately, lower scores.

HOW TO USE THIS BOOK

Since each chapter in this book builds on the preceding one, I recommend that you first read it cover to cover to get the whole picture of the fundamentals of a model golf swing. After you have completed the book, I suggest that you go back to the Grip and Setup chapters and read them again. The reason for this is so you will recognize the importance of how each starting position relates to the other positions in the swing. You will also begin to realize how important the grip and setup positions are to the success of the entire swing.

FIG. I-10. A simple shaft, with a soft handle and protected end, can be one of the most effective teaching aids.

FIG. I-11. An electronic metronome is an effective tool to help understand the concepts of rhythm and tempo.

FIG. I-12. A weighted swing ring can be used to increase both strength and flexibility.

Drills

At the end of each chapter are several drills that will help you incorporate the model information into your swing. You will notice three major characteristics of every drill. First, virtually every drill can be done alone, without assistance. Second, each drill will provide feedback on how well the motion you are striving to achieve is being performed. Finally, all of the drills involve actually hitting the ball. That makes the drills more meaningful and enjoyable.

Swing Aids

Of the many teaching aids we have tried over the years, three have proven to be very useful. The first and most important is a simple golf shaft (fig. I-10). This shaft, which we call the teaching shaft, is a steel shaft at least 38 inches long, without a clubhead. Since the grip end may be struck during some of the drills, it should have a soft grip attached. At the bottom end of the shaft, where the clubhead is normally attached, make sure there are no sharp edges. For safety, this end should be rounded, or a plastic cap placed on the tip.

Good swing mechanics must be accompanied by proper timing and a smooth, flowing tempo. In all of our teaching, we use a metronome to help our students feel the rhythm of the swing (fig. I-11). Any electronic metronome will suffice. Just make sure it can be adjusted to a rhythm in the 1-second range, with an audible beep or click.

The final swing aid is a weighted club. Golf does not require a great deal of strength or flexibility to play well, but if you don't have sufficient amounts of both, your game will suffer. By increasing your range of motion and strengthening your muscles, it becomes immeasurably easier to swing the club properly. Using a weighted club is the way to achieve these improvements. There are several ways to make the club heavier, but we prefer to place a weighted ring on the shaft (fig. I-12). This allows you to carry the weight in your bag, without having to add a special weighted club.

With these simple aids you can perform every drill presented in this book, by yourself or under the observation of a friend, with equal effectiveness.

For the truly serious golfer, it is helpful to have a video camera to record your practice sessions. It is the only sure way to ensure that you are making the right changes in your swing. If you choose to invest in one, make sure that it can be battery driven, has a variable shutter (at least 1/1000), and has onboard, easy-to-use, slow-motion playback.

The Model and Me

To demonstrate the model swing, we use the 3-D performer, which we have termed "the Pro." He has the best characteristics of all of the tour players we have studied over the years. To add a human element to the drills, I will show you how they should be performed. Since the Pro never makes a poor swing, we looked elsewhere to find a subject to demonstrate common swing errors. Since we didn't want to embarrass our students, we used one of our instructors who has an uncanny ability to mimic every swing error we have ever seen.

It should be noted that the swing of the Pro is real and the photos taken of both the drills and the swing errors were actual, dynamic actions. We learned long ago that you cannot stage a swing position, and we have avoided it throughout this book.

Golf Jargon

We try to limit the possible confusion in our teaching by minimizing the use of golf jargon or buzzwords. Some terms, however, cannot be avoided. We will refer to the "target" and "target line" as references (fig. I-13). The target is the point down the range, or course, where

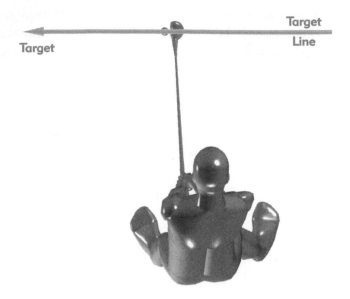

Target

Target Line

FIG. I-13. The target is a point where you aim your shot. The target line (blue) is a line drawn through the ball to the target.

you are aiming. The target line is a line drawn from the ball toward the target.

We will often refer to the necessity of the clubhead and arms to follow an inside path prior to impact (fig. I-14). This is the path that moves inside the target line, produces an "inside-to-square" path, and allows the clubface to strike the ball squarely. Using this path as a reference, any club or arm movement inside or outside this perfect path is termed too far inside or outside. The dreaded affliction "over-the-top" is the act of moving the arms or club outside the proper swing path during the downswing. This produces what we term an "outside-to-inside" clubhead path that produces the all-too-common slice.

FIG. I-14. The model downswing path followed by the Pro allows him to produce the perfect shot, since the clubhead is moving directly at the target at impact (gray). A downswing path that is outside this model path is termed too far "outside" and produces an outside-to-inside clubhead path at impact (blue). A downswing path that is inside this model path is termed too far "inside" and produces an inside-to-outside clubhead path at impact (black).

We take the time to describe these terms because there are many definitions in the golf literature, and we want to avoid any confusion. We also use numerous common golf descriptors such as grip, clubface, face angle, draw, and so on. There is no controversy to these terms, so if you have any questions, ask any experienced golfer or teaching pro.

Gender and Handedness

The limitations of the written word make it impossible to address both men and women as a single unit. We have limited the references to the male gender as much as possible, but in many cases it was unavoidable. We apologize to our female students, recognize the contribution of the

LPGA Tour players who are included in our research, and hope you will understand the dilemma common to all golf writers.

Apologies must also be given to our left-handed students. Although it would have been possible to eliminate all references to left and right in our explanations, it would simply be too confusing (we tried it). We can only hope that switching the two terms will not prove too difficult a task.

BEGINNING YOUR JOURNEY

You should be encouraged to know that the information in the following chapters is based on years spent researching the swings of the best players in the world, and that you have the physical ability to make their fundamentals a part of your swing. If you are serious about improving your game, get your clubs, turn the page, and get ready to play the best golf of your life.

Chapter One

Grip

HANDS ON FOR
A PERFECT SWING

Each component of a model swing is as important as the last. A potentially perfect swing can easily be ruined by a poor setup or grip before the swing even begins. Likewise, a flawed backswing or downswing will ruin the precise preparation made during the preshot routine. In the end, a golf swing is only as strong as its weakest link. If one element of your swing deviates from the standard, you will be forced to make some sort of midswing compensation to atone for it.

The grip is the first and probably the most important building block of the swing. It is also the source of the greatest number of swing errors and compensations. A poor grip renders an otherwise good swing useless. A faulty hold on the club forces you to make an endless series of adjustments that enormously complicates the entire action. And in the vast majority of cases, you will never find a swing that produces a consistent ball flight.

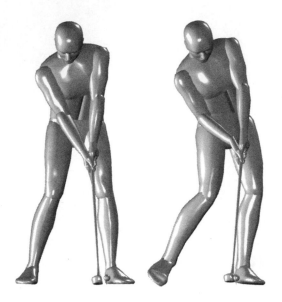

FIG. 1-1. A model grip begins at setup (left), but is configured to produce a successful impact (right). The Pro selects the grip that allows the clubface to square naturally at ball strike.

On the other hand, a perfect grip carries with it a number of very lustrous promises, the most notable of which is that *you are far more capable of returning the clubface to the ball in a perfectly square position* (fig. 1-1). Of course, that is conditional upon your swing also being fundamentally sound, but without a solid grip your efforts to improve are doomed to failure.

If your grip is correct, you can eliminate the hands as a factor when you attempt to sort out the reason for a poor ball flight. And since a mere 5-degree deviation in the clubface angle at impact will send the ball off most fairways, it is comforting to know that your grip is not the culprit when a shot goes astray.

A sound grip also puts your hands and wrists in position to bend and fold just as they should on the backswing and downswing. The movements of the hands and wrists in a model swing are not necessarily complex, but they *are* exacting, and the only way they can perform naturally is with a good grip. If your grip is less than ideal, you will end up fighting the correct hand and wrist action instead of allowing it to occur.

There are other long-term and happy by-products. A sound grip increases your versatility as a shot maker, enabling you to fade or draw the ball at will—without altering the basic grip. It also promotes maximum feel and sensitivity in your hands, so you know where the club is positioned at all stages in the swing. You'll be able to control the club without having to grip it too tightly. And when you place your hands on the club exactly right, you will receive a great deal of feedback when the clubhead strikes the ball.

Suffice it to say, a good grip really is the foundation around which the rest of the swing is built. If your present grip does not exactly duplicate the grip we're about to show you, you *should* change it. This is asking a lot, we know, for experience has shown us that students tend to resist grip alterations more than any other type of swing change (mainly because the new grip feels so unusual the first time it is put into place). The correct grip, however, will begin to feel natural very quickly, and you can feel confident knowing it is the type of grip preferred by the vast majority of top players.

FIG. 1-2. The neutral grip is the most commonly taught hand position. Although it looks good at setup, it does not allow a natural impact to occur.

BAD ADVICE

The majority of instructional programs point to the "neutral" grip as the model for a good swing (fig. 1-2). This grip is formed by placing the hands in a "clapped" position, equally covering the two sides of the shaft. It is completed when the fingers are closed around the handle, with both thumbs placed directly on top. Looking down at address, the *V*s formed by the thumb and forefinger point toward the nose.

This advice has hindered the swings of every

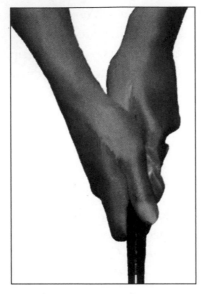

FIG. 1-3. The Pro has discovered that the most productive grip puts both hands in a strong position.

FIG. 1-4. The grip is completed by placing the shaft in the fingers and overlapping the hands.

player who has ever tried it. A few have succeeded, but in a sense they've had to climb a mountain to do it. It is not the grip of choice of the best players in the game, and it isn't the grip for you.

THE GRIP OF CHOICE

Because of the demands of the swing, the best players in the game use a "stronger" rather than a neutral grip (fig. 1-3). The left hand is rotated clockwise to a more active position, the left thumb placed on the right side of the shaft (away from the target).

Likewise, the right hand is also rotated clockwise, allowing the *V* between the thumb and forefinger to point toward the right shoulder.

For both hands, it is critical that the handle is placed in the fingers, not the palms.

FIG. 1-5. The Pro uses the Vardon grip to unite the hands and allow the wrists to move as a single unit.

Finally, the grip is completed by placing the little finger of the right hand on top of the ridge between the left index and middle fingers (fig. 1-4). This grip, popularized by the great English golfer Harry Vardon early in the twentieth century, is the overwhelming choice of the best players today. And for good reason. It reduces the distance between the two hands, attaches them at a single point, and closely aligns the axes of the two wrists with one another (fig. 1-5). All of these benefits allow the two hands to work as a cohesive unit. From a biomechanics standpoint, it is the best grip of all.

There are other grips that have been used with some success. The 10-finger, or "baseball," grip, in which all the fingers of both hands are in contact with the club, is the worst of the options because it limits wrist hinging and discourages the hands from behaving as a close-knit unit during the swing (fig. 1-6).

The "interlocking" grip, in which the little finger of the right hand

FIG. 1-6. The 10-finger grip stifles freedom in the wrists and prevents the hands from performing in a unified fashion.

FIG. 1-7. Although favored by Jack Nicklaus and Tom Kite, the interlocking grip is a most difficult grip to employ correctly.

is laced between the index and middle fingers of the left hand, can be a viable alternative (fig. 1-7). Yet despite its popularity with a few top professionals (Jack Nicklaus is one of them), the tendency among amateurs who use this grip is to place the handle too far into the palms of both hands.

GRIP PRESSURE: NOT TOO LIGHT, NOT TOO FIRM

It is not enough that your hands are positioned correctly. Once your grip is complete, it is imperative that you squeeze the club with just the right amount of pressure. The most common tendency is to grip the club too tightly, thereby inhibiting freedom in your hands and wrists.

We have seen golfers who hold the club too lightly, but they are few in number. For whatever reason—anxiety or perhaps an instinctive need to exert control over the club—far more golfers grip the club too firmly.

YOU CAN'T MANIPULATE THE CLUBFACE

One of the great myths in golf is that you can manipulate the clubface with your hands and forearms to the position you desire during the late stages of the downswing, thereby producing draws and fades at will. For several reasons, it is impossible to control the clubface to such a minute degree, and you're asking for serious problems if you try (fig. 1-8).

We agree wholeheartedly with Ben Hogan, who stated, "Consciously trying to control the face of the club at impact is folly. You cannot time such a delicate and devilish thing. It happens too fast, much too fast." Hogan believed—and our research concurs—that the hands should do little except hold on to the club once the swing has begun.

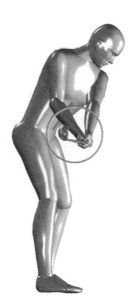

True, the hands serve an active role in that they cock and uncock at the wrists. But consciously rotating them as a means of controlling the position of the clubface is disastrous. You'll either rotate the clubface too far or not far enough; and if you err by only 5 degrees, you'll be playing your next shot from tall grass.

As the clubhead nears impact, it approaches speeds of approximately 100 miles per hour (for a good amateur player). In the context of the entire downswing, you have only 1/5 second to perform a complicated series of acts. First you must discern the position of the clubface, then you must compute how much it needs to be adjusted, then the

FIG. 1-8. Success has taught the Pro that the clubface is controlled by the grip, not by manipulating the hands or wrists.

FIG. 1-9. As impact approaches, the Pro knows that the clubhead is moving too fast, and there is too little time to effectively change the clubface angle. Fortunately, the Proper grip allows him to relax and enjoy the ride.

adjustment message must be transmitted from your brain to your hands, and finally you must rotate the hands the exact amount to make the clubface respond. That's a lot of activity, far too much to accomplish in such a small period of time.

Not to belabor the point, but complicating the task even further is the fact the clubhead effectively weighs as much as 120 pounds through impact, due to centrifugal force pulling it outward away from your hands. Because you are capable of exerting only about 20 pounds of rotational force, altering the clubface position in an exacting manner with your hands is, again, quite impossible. In the end, the hands can do little else but merely hold on to the club (fig. 1-9).

You also should avoid strengthening or weakening your grip at address in an effort to "preprogram" a draw or fade. If your grip deviates

FIG. 1-10. The swing of the Pro moves the hands well forward from setup (blue) to impact (gray). Although this produces great power, it also opens the clubface.

from standard, your hands will not perform naturally on the downswing and you will be wildly inconsistent through impact. It's far better to employ the same standard grip on every shot and attempt to curve the ball by adjusting your stance and body alignment at address.

WHY "NEUTRAL" WON'T WORK

There is a good reason why the better players play with a stronger grip rather than a neutral one. At address, your hands are positioned almost directly in front of you. At impact, however, your hands are considerably farther forward than they were at address—about 5 inches (fig. 1-10). That has the effect of opening the clubface so it is aimed to the right.

Try it and you'll see. Assume your normal address position. Then, keeping the rest of your body still, shove your hands forward toward the target. See how the clubface opens?

Therein lies the problem with a neutral grip (fig. 1-11). It is designed to square the clubface at address. Through impact, however, your hands will not be in position to support and maintain a square clubface. The clubface will automatically open as the hands move ahead of where they were at setup.

The grip used by the best players may appear stronger than what is popularly recommended, but it is designed to ensure a square clubface the moment it meets the ball (fig. 1-12). This the first of several changes that will allow you to depart forever from the 85 percent of the population that slices.

GRIPS MUST BE SIZED CORRECTLY

Clubs generally are sold with a standard-size grip diameter that may or may not fit your hands. If your hands are larger or smaller than normal, you must have new grips installed that are the right size. If your grips are too small, you may not be able to obtain a snug fit when you close your hands around them, and the club can slide out of position without your knowing it during the swing. If your grips are too large, they can restrict action in your hands and wrists, as well as rob you of touch and feel. What is the right size? Take this test. Grip the club with your left hand. Your middle and ring fingers should barely touch your palm. If they curl under the grip and form a layer between your palm and the handle, your grips are too small. If your fingers don't touch your palm, they are too large.

It also is important that your grips be fresh and tacky. If they become hard, worn, or slippery, you'll increase your grip pressure to compensate. It's wise to have new grips installed at the beginning of each season. One of the things that every professional we analyzed insisted upon was grips that fit and were well maintained. They are well

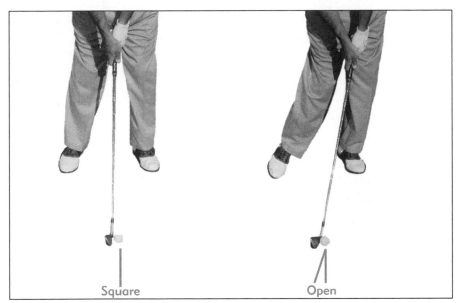

FIG. 1-11. The neutral grip is designed to square the clubface at setup (left). If the proper swing occurs, the clubface will be wide open at impact (right).

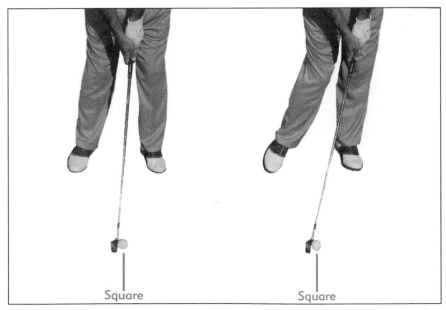

FIG. 1-12. Using the proper grip at setup (left), the swing can be made with the confidence that the clubface will square itself at impact (right).

aware that the grip is the interface between their swing and the club. All golfers should follow their example.

GET IT RIGHT, AND NEVER CHANGE

If the temptation to change your grip becomes great, just remember that any ball-striking problems you experience are the result of incorrect execution of the proper swing fundamentals. Changing your grip to accommodate a swing error will only compound your difficulties. In golf, two wrongs do not make a right, so learn the correct grip at the outset and stay with it.

Your new grip should begin to feel comfortable in a short period of time. The more comfortable it feels, the less inclined you'll be to change it. Practice your grip frequently in your home and office. And check your grip in the mirror occasionally; it helps to inspect your grip from more than one perspective.

THE GRIP DRILLS

These drills are designed to ensure the two critical aspects of the grip: correct hand position and proper grip pressure. Master these drills and you can have confidence that you are ready to begin a model swing.

1. The Model Grip

Regardless of the stage of the swing you are working on, it is best to follow a standard procedure that is repeated every time. That is especially true with the grip. Follow this process every time you prepare to play a shot.

In the finished grip, there is no discerning left from right. Ultimately, your two hands will perform in a unified manner during the swing. But the two hands do occupy different places on the handle of the club, and from a position standpoint they are not mirror images of each other. So it is best to learn how to seat each hand individually.

Step 1. The Left Hand

With the clubhead resting on the ground, steady the club at its very end with the thumb and forefinger of your right hand. Place your open left hand on the club so the handle runs diagonally across your fingers. The handle should intersect the middle joint of your left index finger, travel across the other fingers, and continue up until it intersects the first joint of your little finger (fig. 1-13).

Now close your fingers only (the thumb comes later) so that the fleshy pad to the right of your palm is positioned atop the handle. If the pad is not on top of the club, it's a sign that you've placed the handle too much in the palm rather than along the fingers (fig. 1-14).

Next, place your left thumb on the shaft so it is positioned slightly to the right of center. It is important that your thumb fit snugly alongside the rest of your hand as you perform this last step. As a test, you should be able to secure a tee between your left thumb and hand. The idea is to ensure that your entire left hand be compact when the grip is complete (fig. 1-15).

FIG. 1-13. The initial key is to ensure that the grip is placed in the left fingers.

FIG. 1-14. In the model grip, it is imperative that the handle of the club run below the heel pad of your left hand.

FIG. 1-15. The completed left hand grip should be solid enough to feel as if you could easily swing the club one-handed.

Grip 45

FIG. 1-16. By placing the handle of the club in the fingers of your right hand, you increase your chances of a full, free release through impact.

FIG. 1-17. The completed Vardon grip. The snug appearance of both hands implies unity, strength, and control.

Step 2. The Right Hand

The correct right-hand grip is much more simple, since the left hand is there to act as a guide. Merely place the right hand on the club below the left, lift your right little finger, and slide the hand up the shaft so that the ring finger of your right hand is up against the index finger of your left hand. The handle should run diagonally from the middle joint of the right index finger to the first joint of the ring finger (fig. 1-16).

Now close your right hand, folding the lifeline of your right palm snugly around your left thumb. Your right thumb should be placed just to the left of center on the handle, at the same time pressing lightly against the rest of your right hand. The right little finger should ride atop the ridge between the index and middle fingers of your left hand (fig. 1-17).

Step 3. Check Your Vs

Observe your completed grip. A good check is to place your hands in a mock address position and note where the *V*s of each hand (the crease formed at the junction of the respective thumbs and index fingers) point in relation to your upper body (fig. 1-18). The left-hand *V* should aim precisely at your right ear. The right-hand *V* points farther to the right, directly over your right shoulder.

If the *V*s aren't aimed correctly, rotate the offending

hand(s) bit by bit until they are. You may have to make additional adjustments once you improve your setup position.

2. Grip Pressure

So what is the right amount of grip pressure? Take this test. Assume the correct grip and then have a friend stand opposite you and grasp the end of the club (fig. 1-19). Ask him to pull the club out of your hands. If any slippage occurs, your grip is too light. Next, have him work the club aggressively from side to side. If there is too much resistance on your part—if he is unable to work the club more than a foot in either direction—then you are holding the club too tightly.

A final word about grip pressure. Once you establish a grip that is firm yet sensitive at address, try to maintain the same grip pressure throughout the swing. Golfers very often tighten their grip pressure during the swing in a subconscious effort to maintain control of the club. It isn't necessary. Late in the downswing, you will instinctively increase your grip pressure enough to ensure that you maintain control of the club, though not enough to stifle movement in your hands and wrists.

COMMON GRIP PROBLEMS

The grip is a bit of an enigma. Do golfers select bad grips to accommodate swing errors, or do bad grips produce swing errors? Whether you make it a cause or an effect, a bad grip must be avoided.

FIG. 1-18. The "V" of the right hand points directly over the right shoulder. Although the left-hand "V" is concealed, it is aimed at the right ear.

FIG. 1-19. If your grip pressure is correct, a friend should be able to work the club freely, but not enough to displace the handle from your hands.

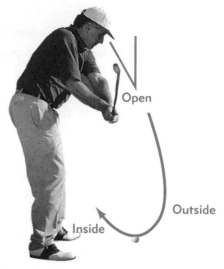

FIG. 1-20. A weak grip—the calling card of golfers who slice. With both "V"s pointed to the left, there is no way to deliver the club back to the ball in a square position without adversely affecting the swing.

FIG. 1-21. One of the major reasons that most golfers fade or slice the ball is the outside-to-inside path that must be produced to accommodate an open clubface.

Problem 1. The Legacy of a Weak Grip

If you are one of the great majority of the golfing population who slice or fade, a weak grip is your worst enemy (fig. 1-20). Since this grip guarantees that you will approach impact with an open clubface, only negative things can result.

The most typical way to square the clubface with a weak grip is to swing on an outside-to-inside path (fig. 1-21). Of course, this only increases the amount of clockwise (slicing) sidespin applied to the ball.

There are several other ways to close the clubface, including releasing the club early or simply slamming the face shut by rotating the forearms just before impact. Whatever the compensation, you won't like the result. Use the "Model Grip" drill to ensure that you are beginning with the proper grip.

Problem 2. Overdoing a Good Thing

Although a slightly strong grip is good, it can be overdone. In an attempt to achieve a quick fix, many slicers use an extremely strong grip to ensure a closed clubface at impact (fig. 1-22).

Whatever the swing flaw, a strong grip is very limiting because it eliminates your ability to let the arms swing freely through impact. Instead, you are forced to "hang on" and not let the clubface close naturally for fear of pulling the shot dead left. This weak push shot is not the one you want when you have a 220-yard carry over water. As with the weak grip difficulty, this problem can be easily avoided by using the "Model Grip" drill.

FIG. 1-22. An overly strong grip may cure an open clubface, but it also promotes a wide range of mechanical errors.

Problem 3. Strangling the Shaft

Developing golfers often feel they must put a death grip on the club. Whether it's a tension problem or an attempt to control the club, this error severely restricts the ability to make a smooth, fluid swing. Use the "Grip Pressure" drill to ensure that the pressure you are exerting is not limiting your improvement.

AVOID THE PROBLEM AND FORGE ON

Bad grip problems can easily be avoided since you can take all the time necessary to get your grip right. Commit to the correct grip, then move on to setup, the second part of a good preparation.

Chapter Two

Setup

WHAT YOU SET
IS WHAT YOU GET

One of the pleasures of watching a skilled player in action is the sequence of events that takes place prior to setting the club in motion. As the final stage of the preshot routine gets under way and he settles over the ball, he executes a series of movements that are fluid yet precise, graceful yet filled with a sense of purpose. The mysterious procedure is systematic and well choreographed, as though designed to achieve some secret yet important goal.

The goal *is* important, yet it is far from mysterious. The painstaking procedure of positioning the body correctly at address serves a number of vital objectives that are at least as important as the swing itself. The quality of every movement in the swing is a by-product of your setup at address (fig. 2-1). That goes for balance, power, timing, rhythm, and mechanics. If your setup is poor, it will negatively affect every one of these factors.

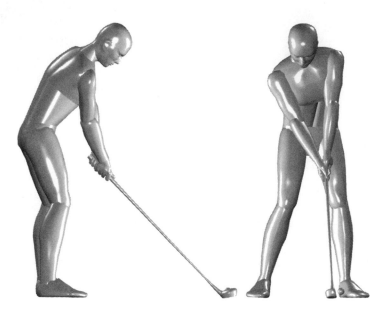

FIG. 2-1. Whether viewed from down-the-target-line (left) or face-on (right), a model setup allows the Pro to look as if every shot will go far and straight.

Many amateurs are surprised to hear of the setup's all-encompassing importance. They may view one or two parts of it as being vaguely significant. They may know that the alignment of the feet affects aim, perhaps, or that ball position helps promote clean club-ball contact. But the setup rarely receives the serious consideration it merits, partly because it is done in preparation for the more exciting act of actually hitting the ball. Yet the setup is an exciting world unto itself. Far from being drab, it requires athleticism to accomplish correctly, plus ample degrees of patience, knowledge, understanding, and practice. The procedure is a dynamic motion, and even the momentary stillness that precedes the beginning of the swing has to it a quality of agility and readiness. It definitely is a "live" aspect of a model swing.

Another reason given for bypassing the setup is that better players seem to set up to the ball in so many different ways. The impression given is that any old setup will do and that only the swing really matters. In fact, this isn't the case at all. The best tour players prepare for the swing in a remarkably similar manner. Just as many good swings possess stylized quirks, the same is true with the setup. Better players with unusual setup positions succeed *in spite* of them, not because of them. The next time you see a good player with an ultrawide stance, keep in mind he has had to work extra hard to construct the swing modifications a wide stance necessitates. On the other hand, if you adopt a model setup position at the outset, the path to ball-striking excellence is shortened immeasurably.

The model setup position promotes a slew of positive swing movements. If your position at address is sound you'll possess

1. the ability to shift and turn freely and fully away from the ball on the backswing, remain balanced, and aggressively move toward the target during the downswing and follow-through;

2. the opportunity to produce a downswing conducted in proper sequence, with the hips leading the way;

3. the ability to achieve an impact position in which the left side of the body is "cleared out" and the right side is working "down and through."

Although all aspects of the setup are important, a few merit special attention. In golf, it pays to understand cause and effect, how positions at the outset influence movement when the swing gets under way. Before moving on to the proper setup procedure, let's examine the primary components of the setup and explore their relevance to the full swing.

BALL POSITION IS CRITICAL

Once you begin the swing, instinct takes over. Your whole being is absorbed in the task of striking the ball, and your body will do whatever

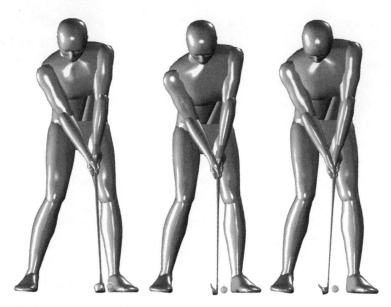

FIG. 2-2. Moving from driver (left) to 5-iron (middle) to 9-iron (right), the setup of the Pro varies only slightly. The small backward shift of the ball is the only indication that a different club is being used.

is necessary to make it happen. Ball position—where you place the ball on the ground in relation to your feet—has an enormous influence on how your body reacts in your attempt to "find" the ball with the club-head. If the ball is positioned correctly, you can swing the club freely and soundly without having to make outlandish compensations with your body. On the other hand, if the ball is stationed poorly, it will demand compensations to ensure an acceptable ball flight.

The proper ball position is forward in the stance. For the driver, the ball is placed directly off the instep of the left foot. As the clubs move from driver to 9-iron, the ball moves back in the stance. The ball position for the 9-iron is slightly less than 3 inches back from the driver position.

One of the many surprises our research found was the small amount

FIG. 2-3. Besides the distance to the ball, the Pro changes the setup only minimally as the clubs shorten from driver (left) to 5-iron (middle) to 9-iron (right).

of movement the ball position made from driver to 9-iron (fig. 2-2). Tradition has always taught that the short irons are played in the center of the stance. As you will see, the best players have good reason not to follow tradition.

The proper distance away from the ball (toe-to-ball distance) is dictated mostly by the length of the typical club (fig. 2-3). The length of the driver produces a distance of about 32 inches, while the shorter 9-iron requires only about 20 inches. This distance can also be affected by numerous body characteristics, including height (taller = closer), shoulder and hip width (narrow = closer), arm length (shorter = closer), and even foot size (larger = closer).

Regardless of its final location, there is little doubt that the position of the ball affects the swing more that any other alignment factor.

THE FEET SET THE TREND

The overall swing goals of the better players can be seen in how they align their feet at setup (fig. 2-4). The left foot is turned out, toward the target, at about 25 degrees. The right foot is positioned straight ahead and slightly forward of the left. It is easy to see what the proficient player is trying to accomplish with this alignment. By turning the left foot out and opening the stance with the right, the feet are positioned to facilitate forward turning on the downswing. Since the power of the swing comes from the big muscles, this foot position ensures a strong contribution on their part.

Surprisingly, this foot position actually limits the body rotation during the backswing by restricting the turn of the hips. This is contrary to most conventional instruction, which stresses maximum backswing rotation. In fact, the better players have discovered that, to apply maximum power, the emphasis must be on downswing rotation. One of the most common problems found in our students is a lack of downswing, not backswing, rotation.

FIG. 2-4. The feet of the Pro show the emphasis placed on allowing the body to turn into the shot during the downswing.

THE SECRET OF THE RIGHT KNEE

One of the better player's secrets is the position of the right knee at address (fig. 2-5). It should be angled in, a bit to the left, so it is nearer the target than your right foot. This adds even greater lower-body support because it prevents you from shifting your weight excessively to the right on the backswing. Your weight must never drift to the outside portion of your right foot. This small but important setup move helps to contain your weight shift within your two feet.

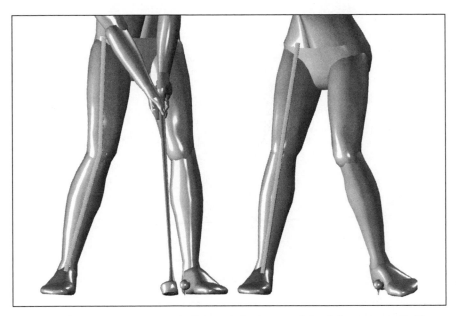

FIG. 2-5. Starting with the right knee shifted toward the left at setup (left), the Pro can control the natural tendency for the knee to move away from the target during the move to the top of the swing (right).

Shifting your right knee toward the target also facilitates the movement of your hips back to the left as you make the transition from backswing to downswing. By preventing excessive lateral lower body movement to the right on the backswing, your hips get a little extra boost when you attempt to move them to the left. It's an efficient trick for expediting the downswing.

KNEE FLEX CONTROLS VERTICAL MOVEMENT

You don't need to browse through an instruction library long before you read something about the body's lateral and rotary movement

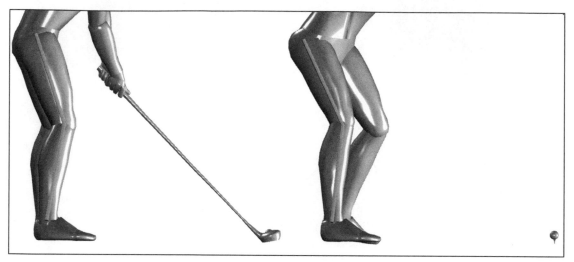

FIG. 2-6. The Pro uses knee flexion to set (left) and control (right) the vertical movement of the swing.

during the golf swing. But every swing has *vertical* motion, too. How else do the hands arrive at the top of the backswing in a position higher than they were at address?

Just as lateral and rotary motion need to be controlled, vertical motion needs to be accommodated smoothly as well. That job is done by the knees (fig. 2-6). At address, your knees must be flexed slightly, positioned to regulate the vertical movement of the trunk, arms, and hands on the back and forward swings. When you swing the club back, up, and around on the backswing, your legs stabilize your body height by maintaining the flexion in the knees. This places your body into a position where the powerful muscles of the legs can be used to help generate clubhead speed during the downswing.

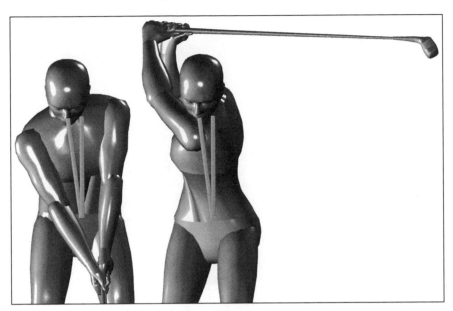

FIG. 2-7. To make the task of leading with the lower body easier, the Pro tilts the upper body away from the target at setup (left), then maintains it to the top of the swing (right).

TILT YOUR SPINE TO THE RIGHT

At the risk of getting ahead of ourselves, the downswing is initiated by shifting and turning your hips toward the target. That movement is made considerably easier by tilting your spine slightly to your right during the setup (fig. 2-7). The slight incline to the right places your hips marginally ahead of the center of your shoulder line. By establishing this tilt and maintaining it throughout the backswing, you'll give your hips the "head start" they need to move properly as you begin the downswing.

Tilting your spine to the right, combined with the angled-in position of the right knee and the overall straightness of your left side, cre-

FIG. 2-8. The effort by the
Pro to get the body behind
the ball is evident at setup.

FIG. 2-9. A comfortable setup
position allows the Pro to round
the shoulders.

ates a unique setup appearance. Observed from head to toe, your body
should resemble the letter *K* in reverse (fig. 2-8). Use this bit of im-
agery in constructing your setup.

SHOULDERS ARE ROUNDED

Golfers are often told to keep their spine absolutely straight during the
setup and swing. That's bad advice. Your spine curves naturally in several
places, most notably near your upper back and shoulders (fig. 2-9). Trying to erase that curve by adapting an artificial posture won't allow your
upper body to perform the way nature intended. What's more, in the
correct setup your shoulders are moved forward, toward the target line,

to accommodate the position of your arms and hands, which are positioned in front of you in order to grasp the club easily. The shoulders-back, spine-straight, military-style posture doesn't allow this to occur.

The shoulders-forward position allows your arms to hang loosely from your shoulders at address. The finished position gives your upper back a rounded, hunched appearance, which is great for the golf swing. The next time you watch a Senior Tour event on television, look at the players as they walk. That rounded-shoulder countenance, first used when they began playing golf, has become a part of their everyday posture!

TWO "MUSTS" FOR THE SHOULDERS

The correct shoulder position at setup involves two factors. First, your shoulders must be tilted, or inclined, so the right shoulder is well below your left shoulder (fig. 2-10). This allows you to move your right arm across your body and join the left so that both hands, the club, and the ball are opposite your left toe at address. The tilt also increases the range of shoulder rotation during the backswing and downswing, enhancing your speed and power potential. The final benefit is that, from this position, you can more readily move your body toward the target on the downswing.

The other "must" is to rotate your shoulder line open so it is no longer perpendicular to the target line. In the finished setup, the shoulders should be aligned slightly to the left of that line (fig. 2-11). This will help you achieve the forward arm and ball placement with ease, and also sets up sound rotation of the body on the back- and forward swings.

FIG. 2-10. By pre-tilting the shoulders at setup, the Pro allows the proper placement of the arms, as well as increasing the contribution of the shoulders during the swing.

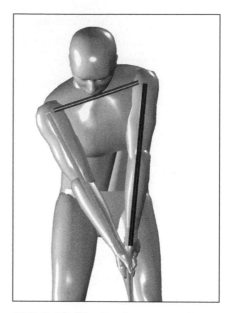

FIG. 2-11. As with foot placement, the Pro begins with the shoulders slightly open to the target to make it easier for the body to turn into the shot during the downswing.

FIG. 2-12. The Pro forms a perfect triangle with the arms, rotated slightly due to the tilt of the shoulders.

FOR THE ARMS, DETAILS COUNT

One of the reasons the shoulders must be positioned so meticulously is to accommodate proper placement of both arms (fig. 2-12). The left arm position is simple: from the face-on view, it forms an almost straight, vertical line from the left shoulder to the handle of the club. The right arm position is a bit more complex. It must reach across your body on a curving path from your lowered right shoulder in a manner that allows the right hand to take its place effortlessly on the handle below your left hand. Ideally, both hands merge together at a point just inside the center of your left leg. By placing your hands forward at the outset, it becomes much easier to return them to a forward position at impact.

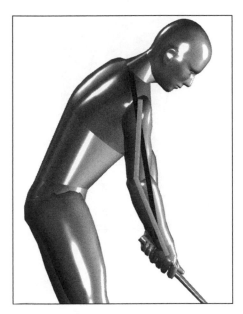

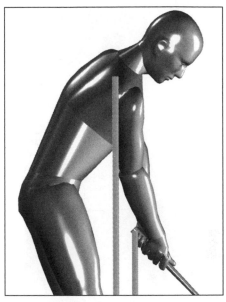

FIG. 2-13. The Pro pre-flexes the right elbow (blue), while maintaining the left arm in a virtually straight position (black).

FIG. 2-14. The Pro positions the arms away from the body to give him room to swing the club. The driver is positioned farthest away from the shoulder center (2"), while the 9-iron is the closest (0").

The correct arm placement doesn't end there. A down-the-target-line view reveals some very important details (fig. 2-13). Note that the left arm is virtually straight, ensuring that a wide swing arc is maintained throughout the swing. The right arm, meanwhile, is flexed slightly at the elbow. That's important because the right arm bends appreciably at this joint on both the backswing and the downswing.

Note also that the left arm is visible from this angle. It must be positioned slightly closer to the target line than the right arm. This will occur automatically if the shoulders are positioned correctly and the proper grip is utilized.

Contrary to popular belief, the arms do not simply hang straight down from the shoulders. Your hands are placed a moderate distance from your shoulders so that the butt of the club is up to 2 inches in

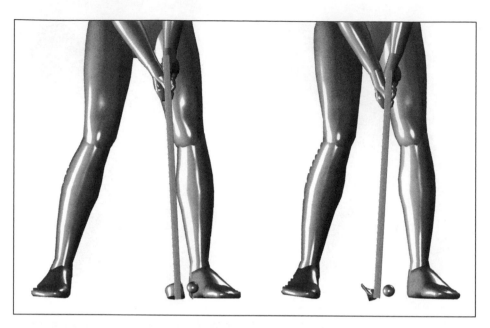

FIG. 2-15. The emphasis on getting the hands forward at setup places the driver shaft almost straight up and down (left). As the clubs move from driver to 9-iron, and the ball is moved back in the stance, the shaft is actually tilted slightly toward the target (right).

front of the shoulder center (fig. 2-14). That gives your arms and hands room to swing back and through once the swing gets under way.

DON'T FORGET THE CLUB

The ultimate objective of a sound setup with the body is to help you move the *club* efficiently during the swing. But it pays to examine the position of the club during the setup, before you move it away from the ball. To that end, the position of the club must satisfy two requirements:

1. From the face-on view, the clubshaft should be in a relatively straight vertical line when the setup is complete (fig. 2-15). Obvi-

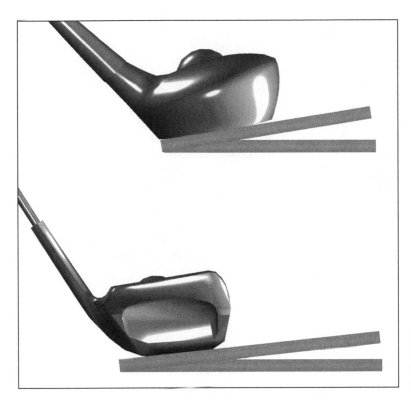

FIG. 2-16. From the driver (top) to the 9-iron (bottom), the Pro sets the clubhead in an upright position.

ously, that means your hands should be positioned directly above the ball. The clubface should be aimed squarely at the target.

2. Contrary to popular belief, the clubhead is not soled squarely along the turf from heel to toe (fig. 2-16). The toe of the club is raised off the ground in a slightly upright position. We'll discuss the reasoning behind this in the Impact chapter, but for now trust us.

BALANCE IS THE FINAL KEY

The final setup key is not about position but *weight distribution*, which plays an extremely important role once the swing gets under

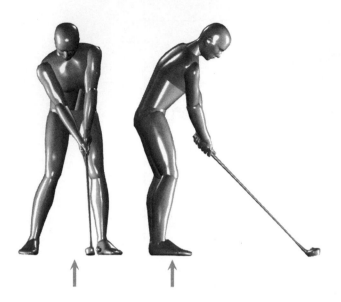

FIG. 2-17. Regardless of the club, the Pro places the body weight evenly between the two feet (left), and just slightly toward the balls of the feet (right).

way (fig. 2-17). Your weight should be distributed evenly between your two feet to facilitate body motion in both directions. You also should place your weight just slightly toward the balls of your feet.

This is the type of posture and balance you want to produce when executing the model setup for golf. Achieve these positions and you will look like a player. A good setup will not guarantee a good swing, but it will *allow* you to make a good swing. In contrast, a poor setup will guarantee you will never make the most of your talent.

YOUR ROUTINE: PUTTING THE PACKAGE TOGETHER

Mastering the precise positions of the setup components is quite a challenge. No less daunting (and important), however, is the ability to integrate the components neatly together as you prepare to perform the swing. The idea is to establish a smooth, well-rehearsed, repeating preshot routine you eventually can perform automatically. Once the routine is mastered, your mind is free to consider other factors of the shot you are facing.

Perform the following setup drills over and over again until they become as natural as sitting down. You should not only practice the routine itself, but also adopt it immediately into your on-course routine. A sound routine requires patience and perseverance, but you'll be surprised how quickly it becomes part and parcel of every shot. Your routine will acquire its own rhythm, and you'll find that cadence creeping into your fast-improving swing and making it even better. In short, you'll wonder how you ever got along without it.

THE SETUP DRILLS

These drills are designed to allow you to consistently produce your own model setup position. Since the setup is stationary, at least for an instant, it is one of the easiest things to get right in the golf swing. And since it will affect everything else you do in your swing, it is well worth the effort to get it right.

1. The Driver

The purpose of the setup drill is to place you in the proper position, every time, without having to think about it. Make the following steps the pattern you follow for every shot and it will give you the confidence that you will begin each swing with the same benefits as the best players in the game.

Step 1

With the club in your left hand, approach the ball from the side and place your feet together so the ball is positioned directly opposite the center of your left foot (fig. 2-18). Assume a comfortable position from the ball (30–34 inches), with both feet pointing directly at the target line.

FIG. 2-18. Start with your feet together with the ball aligned with the
center of the left foot . . .

FIG. 2-19. Pivot your left foot 25
degrees toward the target . . .

Step 2

Turn your left toe out 25 degrees toward the target, while
leaving your left heel in place (fig. 2-19). Try to sense how
this enables you to turn your body toward the target.

Step 3

Take a sidestep away from the target with your right foot
so that your toes are about 2 inches wider than the width
of your shoulders (fig. 2-20). Move your right foot so
that it is 1 inch closer to the target line than your left foot.
Make sure that the foot remains perpendicular to the ball-
target line.

FIG. 2-20. Step to the right with your right foot . . .

FIG. 2-21. Angle your right knee inward, to your left . . .

FIG. 2-22. Then drop your right shoulder downward and let your right hand join the left. Your setup is now complete.

Step 4

Angle your right knee toward the target, allowing your hips to shift forward along with it (fig. 2-21). Your hips also rotate very slightly toward the target, so they are aligned open. Your hips are now in perfect position to make the movements necessary to lead the downswing.

Step 5

Place the club just behind the ball with the left arm so the shaft is vertical from the face-on view (fig. 2-22). Drop your right shoulder downward, at the same time reaching across your body with your right arm and gripping the club with your right hand. Make sure you drop your shoulder enough to accommodate a slight bend in your right elbow. Adjust your position from the ball so that the butt of the club is about 2 inches outside the center of your shoulders.

Your setup is complete! Perhaps it isn't as daunting as we hinted at, after all. But you will need to practice this procedure over and over again until it can be performed subconsciously.

2. The Rest of the Clubs

The posture, positions, alignments, and ball placement just described are for the driver, which is the longest club in the bag and, arguably, the most difficult to control. They raise logical concerns as to how the setup varies for the other clubs in the bag. It's heartening to know, however, that the basic rules of the setup apply to every club, long or short, wood or iron. Part of the beauty of the model swing is its functional efficiency with every club.

There are three closely interrelated factors to consider as you progress through the other clubs. As the clubs move from driver to 9-iron, ball position moves back in the stance, the width of the stance narrows, and the distance to the ball decreases. Once again, you can't perform one part without integrating the other two.

9 iron
5 iron
Driver

FIG. 2-23. As you progress to shorter clubs, your ball position moves farther backward (away from the target) and closer to your feet.

Factor 1. Ball Position The shorter and more lofted the club, the farther back in your stance you must place the ball to ensure optimum club-ball contact (fig. 2-23). Step 1 of the setup drill can be modified to incorporate the required alterations. For the driver, as you already know, the ball is positioned immediately off the center of the left foot. For the 5-iron, the ball is placed opposite the center of the gap between your two feet. For the 9-iron, the ball is placed directly opposite the center of the right foot.

It is interesting to note that the difference in ball position from the driver to the 9-iron is less than the width of two golf balls (about 2.7 inches). Thus, even with the short irons, the ball is played forward in the stance. With the ball positions of the driver, 5-iron, and 9-iron already known, the ball location of the remaining clubs can be estimated.

Factor 2. Stance Width   After you determine the correct ball position relative to your feet-together stance (Step 1) and turn your left foot out (Step 2), you then establish your final stance width by stepping to the right with your right foot (Step 3). The driver stance is the widest. An imaginary line extending vertically upward from the toe of each foot should be 2 inches outside each shoulder. As the clubs become shorter, your stance width becomes increasingly narrow. For the 5-iron, the final stance width should be set at shoulder width. For the 9-iron, the overall stance width is 2 inches narrower than shoulder width. Adjust accordingly with the other clubs.

Factor 3. Distance from the Ball   You stand farthest from the ball with the driver (30 to 34 inches, measured from your left toe) because it is the longest club in the bag. You must stand the proper distance from the ball so the club can perform the way it was designed. With the other clubs, you stand progressively closer to the ball. With the 5-iron, the distance should be between 22 and 26 inches. With the 9-iron, you stand between 18 and 22 inches from the ball.

Don't hesitate to measure the distances for these three clubs precisely using a tape measure. Then, using these firm points of reference, make the necessary slight adjustments with the remaining clubs.

FIG. 2-24. With the ball this far back in the stance, you've no recourse but to slap weakly at the ball with your arms and hands alone.

FIG. 2-25. When your feet are spread too far apart, your lower body becomes "locked" and cannot perform its share of the work during the swing.

COMMON SETUP PROBLEMS

Learning the correct setup requires that you discard forever the positions that feel comfortable in favor of positions you know to be right. That is always a difficult proposition, but it helps to recognize the most common setup errors. In our experience studying and teaching thousands of amateurs, the same setup mistakes tend to occur repeatedly.

Problem 1. Ball Too Far Back in Stance

This is the league-leader in setup blunders. When the ball is positioned too far to the right (fig. 2-24), you can't use your body effectively during the downswing. If you were to shift and turn your hips toward the target as you should, the center point of your swing would be moved so far forward that striking the ball would be impossible. You'd "whiff" it every time. Placing the ball back toward your right foot necessitates a weak, arms-only swing that lacks power.

There's an interesting cause-and-effect relationship here. Does the golfer place the ball too far back because he doesn't know how to use his body, or are his body movements so poor that he must place the ball back in the stance in order to make solid contact? Either way, the solution is the same: you must place the ball farther forward, in the correct position, and *leave it there permanently.* As you train yourself to use your lower body properly, you may hit three or four inches behind the ball for a short period. But it won't take long to make the correct ball position work.

Problem 2. Stance Too Wide

A close cousin to Problem 1, this error adds an extra-wide stance to the ball-back position (fig. 2-25). The wider you spread your feet at address, the more you stifle body rotation on the back- and forward swings. This position promotes over-shifting with the body while slapping at the ball feebly with your arms and hands, resulting in shots that are neither far nor straight.

Problem 3. Foot Faults

There are two frequent errors we see in foot position at address (fig. 2-26). For brevity's sake we'll lump them together here. The errors and their consequences are as follows:

Failure to turn left foot outward This common error restricts lower body rotation, especially through impact and into the follow-through. This is typically done in an attempt to increase the body turn during the backswing, a swing myth that cannot die a fast enough death. To avoid this problem, make sure your left foot is turned out at a 25-degree angle.

Right foot turned outward   Your right foot should be set perpendicular to the target line. If it is flared outward, your hips can turn excessively on the backswing, making it impossible to turn properly during the downswing. This error also allows the body weight to move to the outside of the right foot, making the move into the downswing extremely difficult.

Problem 4. Closed Stance

Placing your right foot farther back from the target line than the left, commonly known as a "closed" stance, is a mistake that is often made knowingly, many times at the advice of an instructor (fig. 2-27). It is usually prescribed as a slice cure, since the inside-to-outside swing path it promotes is meant to counter the outside-to-inside path that causes a slice. But it's a band-aid cure that, in the long run, causes more problems than it solves.

There is no doubt that a closed stance will moderate a slice by artificially changing the swing path of the clubhead. The problems lie in the additional consequences of this action. First, since the closed stance really means you are aiming far right of your target, you will swing your arms way inside the actual target line during the backswing. Experience has taught us that the farther you swing inside the line in the backswing, the farther outside the line you will swing on the downswing. Thus, you will invariably increase your slicing action, worsening your overall swing technique.

In addition, a closed stance severely limits the forward movement as well as the rotation of the lower body during the

Target

Closed   Square

FIG. 2-26. Failure to turn the left foot outward while fanning your right foot outward at address promotes too much hip rotation on the backswing, as well as a destructive lateral slide.

FIG. 2-27. A closed stance, with your feet aligned to the right of the target, sets up a poor back-swing path and an over-the-top move coming down.

downswing. To compensate for this restriction, the upper body is normally used to bring the club around the body. This results in further production of the unwanted outside-to-inside swing path.

Finally, because of the decrement in swing technique and the restrictions placed on the body, the resulting clubhead speed is guaranteed to be significantly lower. The prospect of aiming two fairways to the right, swinging wildly over the top, and trying to hit the ball 50 yards left of where you are aiming should give you some indication that this is not the solution to your slicing tendency. The real solution is to cure the problem, not try to live with it.

PERFECT PRACTICE MAKES PERFECT

One final note. The components of the setup position must be precise. There can be no shortcuts, no relying on what "feels comfortable." Depending on the quality of your setup at present, it may take as long as a month to get the setup down pat, to execute it automatically as you prepare to hit the ball. Use the setup drill and give it the attention it deserves, and you'll be surprised at how easily the rest of the swing falls into place.

ON TO THE SWING

With both your model grip and stance in place, you now look like a scratch player at address. More important, you are prepared to become precisely that. You may still have errors in your swing, but they will no longer be due to your grip and setup positions. You are now ready to conquer your swing flaws from a position of strength.

Chapter Three

Backswing

FUELING A MODEL SWING

The backswing is one of three parts of the golf swing that is slow enough to allow the human eye to distinguish anomalies. And since anomalies are what catch the eye, golfers have concluded that the backswing can be performed in a variety of ways and still be effective. After all, some of the best players in the history of the game, including Ray Floyd, Lee Trevino, and Nancy Lopez, have backswings that can hardly be called classic.

Science, on the other hand, focuses on similarities, not differences. Although this is pretty boring to most people, it does give a better picture of what the majority of people are doing. So, the obvious differences in the clubhead position of a few successful golfers become insignificant when compared to the similarities found in the great majority of the rest of the group of top players. Thus, the traditional takeaways of players the caliber of Nicklaus, Woods, Norman, Hogan, Irwin, Love, Watson, Kite, Whitworth, Sorenstam, Webb, and others more than overcome the few that fall outside what is considered normal.

In addition, since golfers focus on the movement of the club, they fail to notice all of the rest of the parts of the swing. This is understandable since a person has less than 2 seconds to visually evaluate the entire golf swing. During our analysis, it took 10 hours just to get the information on one swing. A painstaking process, perhaps, but it ensured that no part of the swing was ignored.

Despite all of our efforts, the backswing was not a simple analysis. Since this part of the swing occurs at less than full speed, many more errors can be compensated for prior to the downswing. Whereas the computer breezed through other stages of the swing, analyzing data and quickly detecting swing features possessed by virtually all our test subjects, the backswing was more complicated. Yet eventually we were able to identify seven major backswing characteristics responsible for making the best swings "tick" (fig. 3-1).

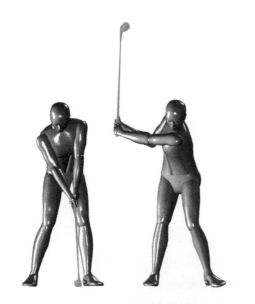

The visual differences in the backswings of even tour players has led most observers to misunderstand the backswing's purpose and to underestimate its importance. Certainly it is well known that the backswing helps you accumulate power through the turning of your hips and shoulders. It is also understood that the backswing imparts rhythm, tempo, and flow, qualities that help the entire motion blend together effortlessly. But the backswing does much more than produce power and flow. It shapes your swing path, ensures good balance, and establishes sufficient swing width and a full arc. Most important, it determines whether you arrive at the top of the swing with the body segments in both the correct position

FIG. 3-1. As the swing begins (left), the Pro executes seven movements that allow him to complete a model backswing (right).

and moving in the right direction to allow the downswing components to fall into place quickly and naturally.

There are other, more subtle advantages. If the backswing is sound, the learning process is shortened drastically because you won't have to perform dicey, midswing compensations in order to make the swing "work." A good backswing promotes repetition and consistency. It makes a sound, powerful downswing much easier to perform. From an aesthetic standpoint, a good backswing gives the overall motion style and distinction. It sets the stage for a full swing that is a pleasure to watch and a joy to experience.

Although many top golfers have succeeded with backswings that are less than perfect, there's little question their paths to excellence would have been shortened had they acquired a more efficient backswing early in their development. Only talent, years of hard work, and repetition have enabled them to groove a serviceable full swing. Lee Trevino, one of the greatest players of all time and possessor of an unusual, self-taught swing, stated recently that if he were starting over again, he would learn a simpler, more conventional swing method because the swing he has took a long time to piece together and requires so much maintenance.

Let's start by examining the fundamental positions and movements and their contribution to a model backswing. Then you can go to work incorporating them into your game.

THE SEVEN CHARACTERISTICS

Statistically, we found numerous backswing positions and movements that were directly related to success in the golf swing. Teaching experience and further analysis has allowed us to determine which of these are the true keys to a model backswing.

Characteristic 1. Arms and Shoulders Behave as a Unit
When the setup is complete, your arms and shoulders form a triangle, albeit a slightly imperfect one due to the shoulder line

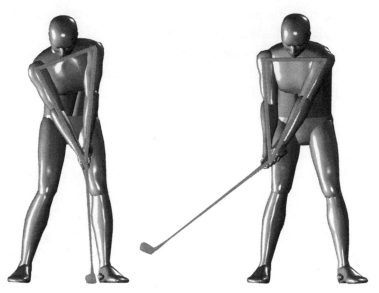

FIG. 3-2. The triangle formed by the shoulders and arms at setup (left) stays virtually intact through the initial third of the backswing (right).

sloping upward when viewed face-on. Where the backswing is concerned, the important point is not the quality of the triangle itself but that *it must remain intact until your hands reach your right pocket* (fig. 3-2). This is the classic one-piece takeaway, which affords the surest, simplest way to start the swing.

In getting the backswing under way, the idea is to keep arm movement to a minimum. Sooner or later, your forearms, wrists, and club will play a role in the backswing, but they join in only when it becomes necessary. Moving your arms as the swing is initiated would severely disrupt the timing of the swing, while serving no useful purpose. During this part of the swing, the arms are moved by the shifting and turning of the body, not by movements in the arms themselves.

When your hands reach your right pocket, the triangle is altered as your right arm begins bending at the elbow. Until this

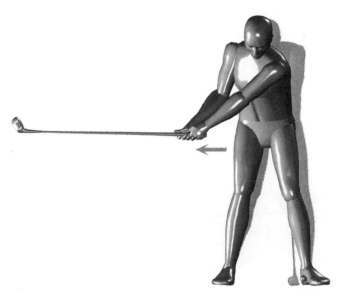

FIG. 3-3. As the Pro moves the club from setup (blue) to a horizontal position (gray), the emphasis is on moving the weight to the right side.

point, however, don't change the relationship between your arms and shoulders. If you swung your arms back while keeping your shoulders motionless (a common backswing mistake), that would alter the shape of the triangle. Likewise, bending either arm at the elbow would also change it. Make sure the arms behave as a unit.

Characteristic 2. The Initial Body Shift

The start of the backswing actually involves two simple, whole-body movements. To begin the swing, you must *shift your entire body laterally to the right* at the same time (fig. 3-3). Shift your hips, shoulders, and head to the right, enough that you feel your weight transferring onto your right leg and foot. The movement is small but pronounced—only about 2 inches total by the time the club is parallel to the ground.

FIG. 3-4. Although the emphasis on the first half of the backswing (left to right) is on moving the weight to the right, the Pro also begins rotating the hips and shoulders.

It is important that you move every part of your body to the right. If your head remained motionless while the rest of your body moved, you'd have a very difficult time shifting your weight onto your right side, and what is commonly called a reverse pivot would result. On the other hand, if you move your head and leave the hips in place, you are restricting the powerful contribution of the lower body. Regardless of the error, it will force you to make compensations that will decrease the quality of your swing.

Although the initial part of the backswing is focused on getting to the right side by moving laterally, some turning of the body does occur (fig. 3-4). Both the hips and shoulders begin the turning action that will be emphasized during the final half of the backswing. This second part of the two body movements is, by far, the most subtle of the two. Overemphasis of this turning ef-

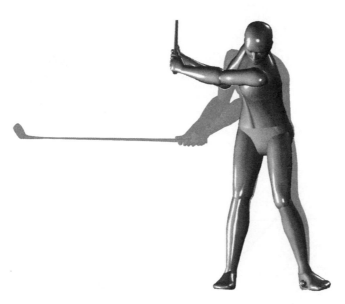

FIG. 3-5. During the second half of the backswing (blue to gray), the Pro shifts the emphasis to turning around the right side.

fort will not only limit the shift off the ball but will place the arms and club in a poor position to properly complete the swing.

The purpose of the initial body movements is to shift the body weight to the right, facilitate the one-piece takeaway of the arms and club, and prepare your body for the dramatic turning that follows.

Characteristic 3. The Turn Begins

Once the shift away from the target is completed (signaled by the clubshaft becoming parallel to the ground) and your weight is placed predominantly on your right side, it is time to transfer the emphasis to turning your body (fig. 3-5). *With your right leg serving as an axis, simply rotate your hips, torso, and shoulders away from the ball.* The turn continues until the backswing is complete.

FIG. 3-6. Although the arms work as a single unit during the first portion of the backswing (left to right), the Pro moves them away from the body (shown by the black extension).

Note that there is no more lateral shifting to the right. That's a critical point because if you continued to shift, your weight would drift so far to the right that you couldn't recover and shift back to the left at the proper time.

It is at this point that you will suddenly feel all the body segments come alive in their effort to complete the backswing. It is the body turn, working in concert with the initial shifting to the right, that eventually will load the swing to its fullest extent and prepare you to perform the downswing.

Characteristic 4. The Disconnection Theory
Much has been said and written about the arms remaining "connected" to your upper body during the swing, but it simply doesn't happen that way in a model swing. Although the arms begin the swing as a unit, they move independently of the

rest of the body (fig. 3-6). To establish the fullest swing arc possible, it is necessary to extend the butt of the club parallel to the target line early in the backswing. Your body, meanwhile, is rotating; with your right hip and right shoulder moving toward your rear, away from the target line. The fact that your arms are moving in one direction and your upper body in another necessitates a bit of separation between your arms and torso.

The overall feeling is one of "reaching" with the clubhead as you extend your arms. You may feel a bit of stretching in your left arm as you achieve this very desirable extension. That's fine. It's a healthy sensation. Think "wide" with your arms as you commence the backswing. Your arms and body will move in sync at the appropriate time and will combine to provide plenty of power and accuracy during the downswing.

It is important to distinguish between the correct "one-piece takeaway" and the incorrect "connection" concepts. It's true that you want to move the arms as a unit at the beginning of the swing. What you want to avoid is bringing the arms with you as you begin the body turn. This arm-and-body connection is one of the most common ways to ensure that you will slice the ball.

Characteristic 5. Clubface Is Slightly Closed

Throughout your backswing, the clubface should remain slightly closed in relation to the target line (fig. 3-7). This closed clubface position is a function of your grip, not of manipulating the club with your hands. If your grip is sound and you perform a one-piece takeaway, the correct clubface position will be at-

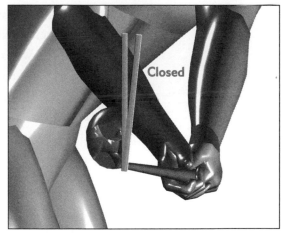

FIG. 3-7. Regardless of the club, the proper grip allows the Pro to produce a closed clubface during the backswing.

FIG. 3-8. The Pro creates most of the wrist cock during the second half of the backswing.

tained naturally and will remain slightly closed throughout the backswing and downswing.

Common sense tells you that a closed clubface, especially in the downswing, will result in hitting all your shots to the left. Notice, however, we did not say that the face was closed at impact. In fact, the better players close the clubface before impact so that it will be square when ball contact occurs. We will explain this apparent contradiction in the Impact chapter.

Characteristic 6. Delay Your Wrist Cock

The hands and wrists do nothing active in the swing during the early stages of the backswing. As noted earlier, the one-piece takeaway is a function of the whole-body turn, complemented by a small lateral body shift to the right.

Once the initial shift and takeaway are complete and your

hands have reached your right pocket, the wrists begin to cock naturally in response to the weight of the club, which effectively increases as it moves away from a vertical position. The cocking occurs gradually and in concert with the turning of your body and swinging of the arms. The great majority of the volitional wrist cock occurs by the time the clubshaft is vertical to the ground (fig. 3-8).

Part of the function of the correct grip is to allow both wrists to cock readily at the proper moment in the backswing. If your grip is sound, you can cock your wrists easily without having to twist your hands to do so.

Characteristic 7. Pace Is Smooth, But Not Slow

For the group of tour professionals we examined (more than one hundred), the average elapsed time from the beginning of the takeaway to the top of the swing was just under one second (.90 seconds, to be exact). That is almost four times longer than it takes to perform the downswing, slow enough to almost be termed "leisurely."

Keeping the .90 seconds in proper context, however, the speed of the backswing is faster than most amateurs realize. The popular teaching adage "You can't swing the club too slowly" just isn't true. If golfers err one way or the other in terms of speed, it is toward the side of swinging the club back too slowly. The backswing must be performed with enough pace to prevent you from manipulating the club, yet slowly enough to maintain a look and feel of smoothness (fig. 3-9).

Never swing the club back so slowly that

FIG. 3-9. Although the Pro takes almost four times longer to move to the top of the swing (blue to gray) as he does to complete the downswing, it cannot be considered a slow pace.

you catch yourself trying to fit the club into a series of positions along the way. The backswing is an athletic motion and requires momentum to be performed properly.

SUMMARY: SHIFT THEN TURN

The seven backswing characteristics are closely interrelated and therefore equal in importance. Each of them must be performed as we describe. Blend them together well and you are sure to arrive at the end of the backswing in an optimum position, primed to execute a beautiful move toward impact.

If there is a thesis statement to keep in mind as you study the seven characteristics, however, it is "Shift Then Turn." Your ability to perform the initial weight shift to the right and then implement the body turn is the most challenging aspect of the backswing, and the part that warrants the most attention and practice. Make it your mantra as you strive to put the backswing package together.

THE BACKSWING DRILLS

Translating the positions and movements into a single continuous motion requires a keen awareness of how your body is behaving at all stages of the backswing. The only way to develop your awareness is to practice. The following drills will speed your efforts to make the seven backswing characteristics part of every swing.

1. Push the Ball
If you're accustomed to starting the takeaway with your hands rather than your arms and shoulders, this drill will cure you fast. Place a basketball directly on the target line, just behind the clubhead (fig. 3-10).

Perform a one-piece takeaway, pushing the ball directly down the target line until your hands are even with your right pocket. At

FIG. 3-10. As you perform the Push the Ball drill (left to right), concentrate on maintaining the triangle formed at setup by your shoulders and arms.

all times, keep the "triangle" formed by the arms and shoulders intact. The resistance provided by the basketball should be felt in your upper arms and shoulders, *not in your hands and wrists.* After your hands reach your right pocket, the club will clear the ball, allowing the clubhead to rise naturally off the ground and permit your wrists to begin cocking. After becoming comfortable with this takeaway, continue the swing to the finish, striking the ball with a normal swing. If done properly, the basketball will roll straight back, down the target line.

The "Push the Ball" drill is a fine way to establish a feeling of unity in your arms and shoulders during the takeaway. That feeling alone will assist you in eliminating excess movement with your hands early in the backswing.

FIG. 3-11. There should be just enough whole-body lateral movement on the first half of the backswing (left to right) for your hips to bump a shaft positioned just outside your right foot.

2. Bump the Shaft

For the two drills that follow, you will need the golf teaching shaft described in the Teaching Introduction. Place the shaft firmly into the ground, straight up and down, so that it is approximately 2 inches from your right hip when you take your setup (fig. 3-11, left). This position is easiest to find with the driver since the shaft will be placed just outside of your right foot. For the shorter clubs, some experimenting will be required to achieve the proper distance.

The first of the two drills is designed to give you both the timing and the tempo of the initial body move off the ball. To begin the drill, assume your setup position (fig. 3-11, left). Initiate the one-piece backswing, allowing your entire body to shift to the right until your hips lightly bump the shaft (fig. 3-11, right). The bump must occur very early in the takeaway, well before the club becomes parallel to the ground or the hands are at hip level.

Once you get the feel of moving off the ball and bumping the shaft at the correct time, go ahead and complete the swing. You have now succeeded in producing the first part of the critical body movement in the backswing.

3. Hug the Shaft

The second of the two body drills is designed to give you the feeling of the pure turning action of the second half of the backswing. Begin the drill by completing the "Bump the Shaft" drill. Once the "bump" has occurred, finish the backswing by turning the hips along the shaft (fig. 3-12). The goal is to avoid pushing the shaft backward, away from the target.

When you're comfortable with this exercise, begin hitting balls. With each swing try to feel the "bump" then "hug" of the shaft. After each effort, check to make sure you have not disturbed the original, vertical position of the shaft.

FIG. 3-12. After bumping the shaft with your hips, complete the backswing without pushing the shaft from its vertical position.

4. Check the Arm, Shaft, and Clubface

This drill is designed to produce the correct arm and club movements during the initiation of the backswing. If done properly, it will prove effective in separating the arms from the body, closing the clubface, and properly initiating the wrist cock.

Take your stance and lay the club you will be using on the ground, the shaft positioned parallel to the target line with the handle touching your right little toe. At the hosel of the club resting along the turf, insert the teaching shaft vertically in the ground so the top of the handle is the same height as your hips (fig. 3-13). Place a tee to mark the position of your right little toe.

Square   Closed

FIG. 3-13. Using the club you will swing in the drill, arrange the club then add the teaching shaft in preparation for a sound backswing check.

FIG. 3-14. Midway through the backswing, the club should be parallel with your stance line and the clubface should be slightly closed (on the ball side from vertical).

Retrieve the club and take your normal setup (with your right little toe on the tee). Perform the early part of the backswing, then freeze when the clubhead reaches the top of the shaft that is sticking out of the ground (fig. 3-14). Check for three factors:

Factor 1   Your hands and the club should be directly above an imaginary line drawn along your right little toe and the teaching shaft.

Factor 2   The club shaft should be parallel with the ground, transported there by a combination of initial whole-body shift and turn, arm swing, and wrist cock.

Factor 3   The clubface should be slightly closed. By that we mean the angle between the clubface and the horizon should be slightly less than 90 degrees, tipped toward the target line.

If you've satisfied those conditions, your backswing checks out great. Go ahead and hit balls this way, just nicking the handle of the teaching shaft with the clubhead during the backswing. If you hit the shaft hard you are swinging the club excessively to the inside, and if you miss the shaft entirely you are swinging excessively to the outside. With practice, you should be able to nick the teaching shaft consistently. On the downswing, of course, you will miss the shaft entirely due to the swing arc becoming narrower.

5. *Produce Wrist Cock*

This drill is designed to provide a sense for when the wrist cock should be emphasized during the backswing. Begin from your normal setup position (fig. 3-15, left), start your swing, then stop when your hands reach your right pocket (fig. 3-15, middle). If done correctly, your weight should be on your right side, with the club pointing at your belly button. Without moving your body, lower your arms and place the club on the ground. Now begin the swing again, with the emphasis on producing as much wrist cock as possible, as fast as possible (fig. 3-15, right). After a few practice swings, try hitting balls with this drill.

If performed correctly, you should feel the stress on the wrists as they attempt to bring the club upward. After some practice, there should be no difference in ball distance between these swings and your normal shots.

6. *Feel the Backswing Tempo*

The first five drills are designed to produce the correct movement at the right time (timing). This particular drill is designed to give you the feeling of the correct tempo or pace of the backswing. The goal is not to try to produce any positions during the backswing,

FIG. 3-15. Early in the backswing (left to middle), there should be no conscious effort made to cock your wrists. Only when your hands reach your right pocket (middle) should you attempt to cock the club upward. Beginning from this position, emphasis on wrist cock should be made as the backswing is completed (right).

but to complete the swing at the correct pace. Using the teaching metronome described in the Teaching Introduction, set the tempo at exactly 1 second. Take your setup, concentrate on the beat, and visualize your swing moving from setup to impact at the proper tempo. Turn off the metronome, take your setup position, and perform the swing trying to make ball contact at the same pace you heard from the metronome. Since only the backswing occurs at less than full speed, you will have to adjust this to achieve the proper swing tempo.

EASY SOLUTIONS

The fact that we spend more time changing the backswing problems of our students points to the importance we place on this part of the swing. Experience has taught us two things about the backswing. First, you will pay dearly for any error you make in this part of the swing. Not only are you forced to compensate for the error by making another swing change, but you also lose both distance and accuracy in the process. Second, because the backswing occurs at less than full speed, changes can be made fairly easily. So golfers are fortunate in that the most important part of the swing is the easiest to fix.

COMMON BACKSWING PROBLEMS

There are countless possible errors that can be created in the backswing, and we have seen most of them. The following, however, are those that are either most common or most disruptive in nature.

Problem 1. Poor Shift and Turn

The most frequent backswing problem is poor execution of the lateral body shift to the right in the early stages of the takeaway (fig. 3-16). Either there is no shift at all or (more likely) it occurs too late. Lack of a proper body shift significantly decreases distance off the tee because you never get in position to use the power of the whole body. A sure sign of a poor initial body shift is a desire to place the ball farther back in your stance in order to make solid contact.

The immediate remedy for an ill-timed, incomplete, or excessive body shift to the right is to perform the "Bump the Shaft" and

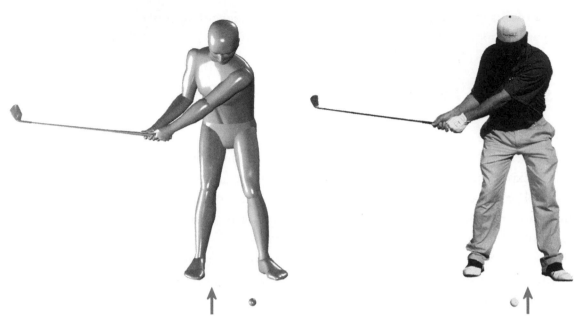

FIG. 3-16. The Pro has made a full body shift to the right, moving the weight onto the right side (left). The arms of the student (right) have moved the club away from the ball, but the lower body has remained frozen in place, producing little weight shift to the right. This is a recipe for disaster.

"Hug the Shaft" drills. More information on the consequences of an improper body shift can be found in the next two chapters.

Problem 2. Bad Connection

Another serious error is failing to separate the arms from the body during the initial stages of the backswing (fig. 3-17). Too many golfers bring their arms along with the body as it rotates, resulting in an arm-and-club position that is too far inside the target line. This excessive, inside swing path is one of the most common problems in the developing golfer, and one of the most destructive.

Remember, the farther *inside* you transport the club on the

FIG. 3-17. The Pro separates the arms from the body during the first half of the backswing (left). The student keeps the arms and body connected, producing an excessively inside path. From here, the student will loop the club "over-the-top" during the downswing, producing a slice and/or pull.

backswing, the greater the tendency to swing "over the top" and move the club to the *outside* on the forward swing. The outside-to-inside swing path produced by this move is the most common contributor to slicing.

The "Arm, Shaft, and Clubface" drill was designed to give you the ability to correct and avoid this problem.

Problem 3. Rolling the Clubface Open

Some swing errors are easier to compensate for than others. One backswing flaw that is impossible to recover from is rolling your wrists clockwise on the backswing, which opens the clubface early in the swing (fig. 3-18).

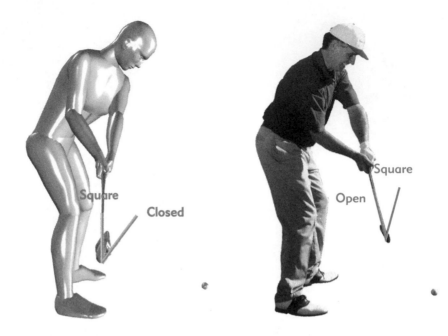

Square   Closed   Open   Square

FIG. 3-18. The Pro maintains control of the clubface, keeping it slightly closed during the backswing (left). By rotating the clubface open early in the backswing (right), it is very unlikely to be returned to the ball in a square position.

This is another slice-producing move. Usually the clubface will remain open for the rest of the backswing, throughout the downswing, and all the way to impact, producing a shot that curves wildly to the right. The only compensation available is to slam the clubface shut at the last instant, producing a shot that may go anywhere, depending on the timing of the maneuver.

The solution is to make sure your grip is correct, then avoid any undue manipulation of the hands during the entire backswing. Perform the clubface check described in the "Arm, Shaft, and Clubface" drill and commit the feeling to memory.

FIG. 3-19. A one-piece takeaway places the club in the model position halfway through the backswing (left). If the wrists are cocked too early (middle) or too late (right), the ability to time the swing is complicated enormously.

Problem 4. Wrists Cock Too Early or Too Late

Improper timing of your wrist cock, whether early or late, is asking for trouble (fig. 3-19). Too early a wrist cock violates the one-piece takeaway trend discussed previously. This error allows the wrist action to "get ahead" of the rest of the swing, which tends to throw off the timing of the movement. This can result in an early release of the club or simply a lack of swing speed at impact.

Delaying your wrist cock tends to delay the completion of the backswing. This typically results in overswinging and allowing the arms to fall behind. Although a delayed wrist cock is capable of producing additional power and is utilized by most long drivers, the average golfer doesn't possess the strength to maintain control of the club.

Proper timing of the wrist cock is critical. If this is your weakness, the "Push the Ball" (early wrist cock) and "Produce Wrist Cock" (late wrist cock) drills will give you the feel of when the arms and wrists should be involved in the backswing.

Problem 5. The Forever Backswing

Some golfers have backswings that are so slow that they never allow the club to become part of the swing. Instead, they try to control the club every step of the way, resulting in a contrived, jerky motion. Use the "Feel the Backswing Tempo" drill to ensure that you are swinging, not manipulating, the club.

IS THAT ALL THERE IS?

You may be curious as to why we ended the discussion of the backswing before the top of the swing was reached. The simple fact is that a critical movement occurs between the end of the backswing and the top of the swing. We call this movement the "transition," and it embraces the most dramatic moment of every good swing. It is the motion that separates the good player from the hacker, and deserves a chapter all its own.

Chapter Four

Transition

THE MAGIC MOVE

If there is an aspect of the tour player's game that inspires a sense of awe and wonder, it is his ability to crush the ball 300 yards or more with such grace and seeming lack of effort. The distance these pros are able to achieve (with accuracy as well) can be unfathomable to the average golfer. It obviously is not a product of sheer size or strength since many pros are small physically yet capable of hitting the ball inordinate distances. The casual golfer can attribute this skill only to equal parts skill and magic.

In fact, there *is* skill involved and some magic too, though the "magic" is attainable by anyone possessing average strength and coordination. It all can be traced to the transition move, the critical series of events that occur as the backswing evolves into the downswing (fig. 4-1). If you're looking for the greatest source of power in golf, this is it, hands down.

FIG. 4-1. The transition in the golf swing occurs from the time the club is vertical (blue) and the top of the swing (gray).

Viewed from afar, the transition move is what gives a great golf swing its undeniable sense of rhythm, grace, and flow. And when you experience it for yourself, the effect is even more astonishing. You'll hit the ball farther than you ever thought possible, with less effort than you probably are applying now. And the accompanying rewards of improved accuracy and greater consistency aren't bad either.

YOUR GREATEST CHALLENGE

Most of the fundamentals of a model swing are relatively easy to learn. The correct stance, posture, and grip, for example, are static, fairly uncomplicated positions that are readily assimilated into your preswing routine. They require careful study at the outset, followed by periodic checking to ensure that you continue doing them correctly, but for the most part they are easy to repeat once you commit them to memory. Even when you set the swing into motion, the proper backswing movements, though precise and regimented, are well within the grasp of anyone with average motor coordination.

The transition move—the change of direction from the backswing to the downswing—is a bit more complicated. It also is the one movement in golf in which the world-class ball striker and the average golfer differ dramatically. If there is an aspect of the full swing that can be labeled the chief determinant of distance, accuracy, and consistency, the transition move is it.

Every athletic endeavor that involves striking, throwing, or kicking requires a transition move of some kind. The term "transition" is used to describe how an athlete uses the large segments of the body to generate great speeds in the smaller segments. This sequence can be seen in a wide variety of motions including baseball pitching and hitting, the tennis stroke and serve, the hockey slapshot, and, of course, the golf swing. In every case, the large muscles attached to the large segments exert tremendous power to stop the backswing movement of the smaller segments (along with the ball, bat, racquet, stick, or club) and propel them toward impact.

To receive maximum benefit from the transition, a number of things must be done. First, the large segments should be in contact with the ground for a firm base of support. Second, the entire body should be moving away from the intended target when transition begins so as to increase the stretching action. Third, the large muscles attached to the large segments should be stretched when transition begins for maximum power production. Finally, the transition must begin with the large segments moving toward impact, then sequentially bringing the smaller segments along with them.

Since everyone has thrown a ball, it is easy to sense the chain reaction of movements that occur as you prepare to release the ball toward the target. First, experience tells you that the throw must begin with the feet planted firmly on the ground. Second, you shift your weight to the back foot as you move away from the target. Third, as your weight shifts back, you turn the hips and shoulders, winding up the large muscles of the lower body and trunk. As transition begins, your torso unwinds first, then your shoulders, and finally, the stage is set to move the arm and actually throw the ball. The act is simple, almost instinctive, and it is easy to sense the physical movements that transpire. The next time you go to the practice range, throw a ball down the range and you'll see what we mean.

As you would expect, the elite athletes perform the transition best. The most impressive example of this came from a high-speed sequence we shot of the great fastball pitcher Nolan Ryan. During Ryan's delivery, his entire body faced the batter, all of the major muscles stretched to the limit. The ball, however, remained stationary, if only for an instant. Another moment later, the ball left Ryan's hand at over 100 miles per hour. This same progression, although not as dramatic, can be seen in any throwing sequence (fig. 4-2).

FIG. 4-2. Although most of the pitcher's body is well into the delivery process, the ball remains stationary. For a superior performer, the ball is accelerated from zero to 100 miles per hour during the last instant of the pitching motion.

The transition move in the golf swing bears many similarities to throwing a ball, but in several respects it is more complicated and less natural to perform. That's because the golf club is the longest implement with the smallest hitting area in sports. In addition, the body is not well suited to produce the unusual path that the swing must follow. Swinging a golf club properly is in itself not an intrinsic, instinctive act, and the correct transition move is more difficult to discern—at least at first. Yet if you are to reach your full potential, you must learn to perform it well.

ANATOMY OF THE TRANSITION MOVE

Golf would be simplified enormously if all you had to do was place your body and the club in a mechanically perfect, rock-steady position at the top of the backswing and then swing away from there. A backswing wouldn't even be necessary. You could merely lift the club into place, check that your positions were sound, and then move all your body parts forward all at once, confident that a perfect swing was preprogrammed.

The golf swing doesn't transpire that way, of course, nor does any truly athletic movement in any other sport. To again borrow the analogy of throwing a ball, imagine a baseball pitcher reaching the top of his windup and then, keeping his lower body stationary, flipping the ball forward with his arm alone. He'd throw a pretty feeble pitch. He needs a dynamic transition move, a cooperative movement between his upper and lower body that accumulates energy, stores it, then unleashes it with tremendous speed and force.

To set the stage for a correct, powerful downswing, it is necessary for the upper and lower body to move in opposite directions just before the downswing actually gets under way (fig. 4-3). That's what the transition move is all about. A moment before your torso, shoulders, and arms complete their journey to the top of the backswing, the lower body, led by the hips, begins moving and rotating toward the target.

Performed the right way, the transition move accomplishes several objectives. First, it "loads" the swing dynamically. The large rotational muscles in your trunk are stretched like a series of powerful rubber bands. So, too, are all the muscles running from your torso to your arms. They become stretched and taut, ready to snap into action to provide great speed and strength.

Second, the accompanying weight shift from the right foot to the left foot that happens when the lower body moves forward provides a stable base of support for the unwinding of the upper body that occurs a moment later (fig. 4-4). It enables you to swing all-out with your shoulders, arms, and hands without risk of losing your balance or wasting energy.

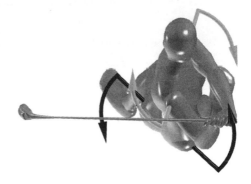

FIG. 4-3. As the upper body (blue) continues to rotate to the top of the swing, the Pro begins rotating the lower body (black) toward the target.

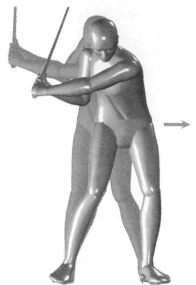

FIG. 4-4. In addition to the hip turn, the Pro also begins to shift the lower body toward the target during the transition (blue to gray).

FIG. 4-5. From the end of the backswing (blue) to the point where the right elbow reaches hip height, the Pro uses transition to get the lower body out of the way so that the arms can follow an inside path.

Finally, the initial move forward with your feet, legs, and hips sets up a chain reaction of movements in the upper body that allow you to transport the club forward along the proper swing path.

Although the main purpose of transition is to produce power, it has the nice residual effect of allowing the correct swing path to occur. One of the major reasons most golfers fade or slice the ball is because they're unable to move the lower body out of the way of the upper body and club. It is obvious that if the hips are in the way during the downswing, the arms and club cannot follow the inside path required to hit the ball straight. Instead, the lower body is an obstacle that forces the arms and club outside, producing the dreaded slice. The transition serves to remove this obstacle by initiating an early power body shift toward the target (fig. 4-5).

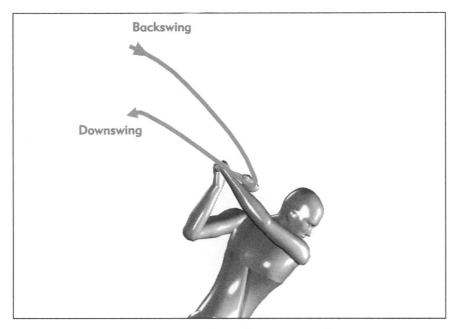

Backswing

Downswing

FIG. 4-6. The transition allows the Pro to let the club fall backward, away from the target line at the top of the swing.

How the clubhead itself moves is important in generating the proper swing path. The transition helps to produce what we call the proper "fall of the club," in which the clubhead actually moves away from the ball as it nears the top of the swing (fig. 4-6). This automatically moves the clubhead onto an inside path during the downswing. The fall of the club is so important that, if done properly, it single-handedly eliminates problems related to swing path.

HOW TO LEARN THE TRANSITION MOVE

The challenge of learning to uncoil your lower body while the upper body is still rotating to the top of the backswing is an awesome one to most golfers. The concept of moving segments of your body in different directions simultaneously is difficult to grasp, let alone perform—at least at first. In a way it's like asking a child to rub his stomach in a circular motion with one hand while patting the top of his head with the other. The child will appear confused initially and fail at first attempts, but will eventually learn to do it.

We believe there are only three sound and lasting ways to learn the transition move. The first is to simply observe the best players in action, using the visuo-motor rehearsal program outlined in the Timing and Tempo chapter. Although all players on the major tours perform the transition move well, we recommend you select a few whose swings are noted for their powerful moves toward the ball. You'll also find it helpful to videotape your favorite players as they perform on television, so you can play the tape back at a quiet time, when the learning environment is ideal.

Next, practice the drills that follow. Of all the drills we have experimented with in teaching, these are by far the most effective in teaching the correct transition move. They are designed to ingrain both proper feel and mechanics.

Finally, *practice.* We've discussed the importance of practice already, but it can't be overemphasized here. Some aspects of the swing "take" faster than others, and perfecting the transition move probably will take longer than most. Be patient, and persevere.

THE TRANSITION DRILLS

These drills are designed to give you the feeling of getting the lower body to begin the downswing while the upper body continues to complete the backswing. It is a movement that will feel very unusual if it is not already a part of your swing. Once you master it, however, your game will be transformed.

FIG. 4-7. Begin by placing the teaching shaft outside your right foot.

FIG. 4-8. Early in the backswing, bump the shaft with your right hip, then slide along the shaft as the backswing is completed.

1. Bump, Hug, and Go

This drill is a continuation of the "Bump the Shaft" and "Hug the Shaft" drills presented in the Backswing chapter. As in those drills, place the teaching shaft firmly into the ground, straight up and down, so that it is approximately 2 inches from your right hip when you take your setup (fig. 4-7). This position is easiest to find with the driver, since the shaft will be placed just outside of your right foot. For the shorter clubs, some experimenting will be required to achieve the proper distance.

As you begin the backswing and shift your weight to your right side, allow your right hip to move laterally far enough to give the shaft a light bump as the club becomes horizontal to the ground. At this point, your right hip should move no farther to the right. It

FIG. 4-9. During the transition, move and turn your hips away from the shaft while continuing to rotate your upper body away from the ball.

FIG. 4-10. Through impact, the full extension of your arms and the powerful lateral movement of your lower body produces a stretching sensation in your torso.

should simply hug the shaft until the club reaches a vertical position in your backswing (fig. 4-8).

At the moment the club becomes vertical to the ground, move and rotate your hips *smoothly* away from the shaft, directly toward the target (fig. 4-9). Your goal is to create as wide a gap as possible between your hips and the shaft while the upper body continues rotating to the top of the backswing.

Swing down and through the ball, noting all the while the sensation of the transition move. If done properly, you will feel stretching in the muscles in your trunk and those connecting your trunk and arms (fig. 4-10). More important, you will begin to feel the power flow from the large leg and trunk segments to the arms and club.

As with all of our drills, you can actually strike the golf ball. At the beginning, however, you may want to eliminate the ball so that you can concentrate on the transition. Then, when you feel comfortable with the move, add the ball and prepare yourself for an improvement in distance.

Because you are partially preoccupied with trying to hit the ball, and your hips are out of view, it may be difficult at first to tell whether your hips are moving a sufficient distance laterally away from the shaft and whether they begin moving back toward the target at the right time. We strongly recommend having a friend stand opposite you to monitor your performance.

FIG. 4-11. Begin the Step and Go drill by addressing the ball normally.

2. Step and Go

If you have any baseball experience, you will like this drill. On the practice range, place a ball on a low tee, then follow this procedure:

Step 1

Using any club (short irons are easier), set up to the ball in a normal manner (fig. 4-11).

Step 2

As you begin the backswing by moving your entire body onto your right side, pick up your left foot and slide it toward your right (fig. 4-12). Make sure that you turn your shoulders so that your left shoulder is over your right foot.

Step 3

As the club reaches the vertical position, click your left heel on your right heel. Without touching the ground, drive the left leg and hip toward the target

FIG. 4-12. As the backswing begins, take a step to your right with your left foot.

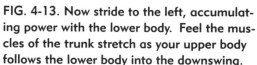

FIG. 4-13. Now stride to the left, accumulating power with the lower body. Feel the muscles of the trunk stretch as your upper body follows the lower body into the downswing.

FIG. 4-14. Through impact, you should be able to hear the club tearing through the air.

as the shoulders and arms complete their backswing motion. You will feel the powerful trunk muscles stop the shoulder rotation, and pull the arms and club into the downswing (fig. 4-13).

Step 4

Finish the swing by allowing the trunk and arm muscles to stretch and then unwind into the downswing (fig. 4-14). Don't rush the transition. Allow the power to build during this portion of the swing and continue through impact.

If performed properly, you should hear the clubhead "whoosh" at the bottom of the swing. Like cracking a whip, the big muscles

FIG. 4-15. Hold the club horizontal to the ground. When swinging a weighted club, begin the motion slowly.

transfer all their power to the end of the club, creating enormous velocity.

As with the "Bump, Hug, and Go" drill, you may want to begin without a ball until you are comfortable with the new power you are creating in your swing.

3. Weighted Club Transition

Using the weighted club described in the Teaching Introduction, begin from the setup position. Start the swing, then stop when the club is horizontal to the ground (fig. 4-15).

Slowly resume the swing, using the entire body to begin the move to the top.

When the club is vertical to the ground (fig. 4-16), prepare to

FIG. 4-16. Using the whole body, swing the club away from the target.

FIG. 4-17. When the weighted club begins to stretch the muscles of the trunk, you should begin to rotate the lower body toward the target.

reverse the club movement by rotating the hips, then the shoulders, then the arms in the opposite direction (fig. 4-17). Once the transition has been completed, keep swinging and allow the momentum of the club to carry you into a full follow-through.

If your goal is to increase flexibility, go slowly and allow your muscles to stretch and pull the club around. If strength is your goal, pick up the pace and make an effort to move the club faster as you bring it around.

After several swings, take an unweighted club and hit balls trying to produce these same swing feelings.

COMMON PROBLEMS, EASY SOLUTIONS

Some transition problems are caused by poor preparation, some by poor execution, and some by external reasons. Regardless of the causes, it must be addressed if you are to reach your potential in your game. The good news is that the cures are easy to assimilate into your swing.

COMMON TRANSITION PROBLEMS

If learning the transition move proves problematic over a long period of time, you probably are committing one of five mistakes. Two of the errors are rooted in poor preswing fundamentals and can be detected and cured by yourself. The third and fourth result from poor execution of the transition move itself and will require observation from a friend. The final problem— lack of body strength or flexibility—is inherent and can be improved upon with an exercise or flexibility program.

Problem 1. Ball Too Far Back in Stance
In the Setup chapter we discussed ball position and how it influences ball flight and quality of club-ball contact. But we've saved another aspect of ball position for now, for it has a special meaning related to the transition move. Simply put, if your ball is positioned too far back in your stance, you will instinctively perform the transition move poorly.

When the ball is stationed too far to the right in your stance, you'll be discouraged from shifting your hips toward the target as you attempt to make the transition move. That's be-

FIG. 4-18. If the Pro placed the ball back in his stance, then made the perfect swing, he would embarrass himself by missing the ball completely.

FIG. 4-19. With the ball forward, the Pro (left) makes a powerful move into impact by shifting the weight to the left side. The student is hanging back on his right side (right), the product of the ball being positioned too far back in his stance.

cause moving your hips laterally to the left effectively moves the center of your swing forward, toward the target. The clubhead will reach the lowest point of its arc more toward your left foot than your right. In fact, if you played the ball back in your stance and made a perfect swing, you would miss the ball entirely (fig. 4-18).

When the ball is positioned toward your right foot at address, it becomes necessary to hang back on your right side on the downswing in order to hit the ball solidly (fig. 4-19). Hanging back is a sure sign the transition move hasn't taken place.

Review your ball position and make sure it is far enough forward to accommodate the transition move.

FIG. 4-20. Because the student assumes a weak grip at address (left), it eliminates his ability to get the hands in front of the ball as impact approaches (right). It's almost a sure bet he'll return the clubface back to the ball in an open-face, slice-producing mode.

Problem 2. Grip Is Too Weak

It is crucial that your hands be placed on the club in a manner that allows you to rotate the clubface to a square position at impact. If your grip is too weak—your left or right hand rotated too far counterclockwise on the shaft—your hands won't be in position to naturally square the clubface late in the downswing (fig. 4-20).

The consequences of a weak grip are well known to the experienced player, but its disastrous relationship with an aggressive transition move are not. When you shift your hips toward the target late in the backswing, it places a strong onus on the hands to play catch-up on the downswing. If your grip is weak, the hands

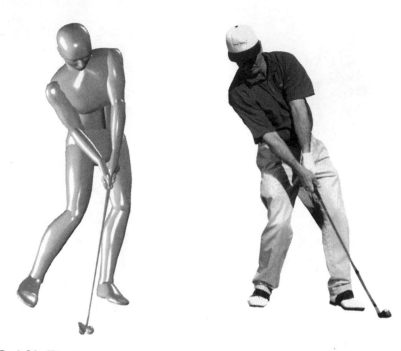

FIG. 4-21. The Pro uses the transition to move most of the body weight to the left side at impact (left). The chief consequence of a poor transition move is hanging back on the right side (right). The end result is a weak, glancing blow at impact.

will never properly join in with the arms, shoulders, and lower body. The clubface will be open at impact, and a push and/or slice will result.

Inspect your grip periodically to make sure it is consistent with the grip we described in chapter 1.

Problem 3. *Hanging Back on Your Right Side*

The transition move requires a shifting of the weight to your right side early in the backswing, marked by the lateral move with your hips. If you allow the hips to shift *too far* to the right, however, the transition move becomes impossible to execute (fig. 4-21). This over shift can be caused by too much lateral move at the beginning of the backswing, but it is usually due to continuing to shift the hips to the right during the second half of the backswing (when they should only be turning). Regardless of the cause, you simply cannot recover in time to shift the hips back to the left. When it comes time for the upper body to uncoil on the downswing, your lower body won't be in position to support that movement. Moreover, the dynamic resistance between the upper and lower body created by the transition move won't be created at all. You'll lose power, accuracy, and consistency.

If you fall in this category, have someone watch as you perform the "Bump, Hug, and Go" drill. Make sure your hips are moving laterally to the right the correct distance on the backswing and that they move aggressively away from the shaft when you perform the transition move.

Problem 4. Upper-Body Dive

There are many movements golfers make to compensate for poor swing mechanics. One of the worst, and most frequent, is what we call the "upper-body dive." If the lower body isn't used at all during the swing, a player tends to move away from the target with the upper body during the backswing, then dive forward and down with the upper body during the downswing (fig. 4-22). This move can actually be very effective in getting the hands ahead of the ball at impact, resulting in solid ball contact. In fact, some band-aid teachers actually use this move to make rapid improvements in ball striking.

Unfortunately, the upper-body dive will always produce a downswing that is outside the desired swing path, resulting in a shot that starts left and slices back to the middle. It is also characterized by deep divots that are pointed to the left of target.

We have seen relatively decent players survive with an upper-body dive because it can produce solid ball contact as well as acceptable distance. Eventually, however, they seek professional help due to the limitations caused by the poor ball flight characteristics.

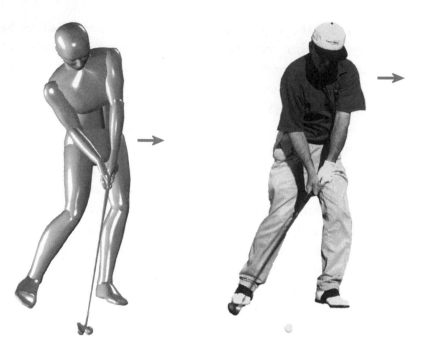

FIG. 4-22. The transition allows the Pro to lead the downswing with the lower body (left). Poor use of the lower body transfers the onus to the upper body (right). The result is an ungainly "dive" and deep divots aimed to the left.

If the dive is part of your game, work on the transition with the "Step and Go" drill. Make sure that you move your hips to the right at the beginning of the backswing. If you still have difficulty, simply begin the drill with your feet together until you get the feel of leading the transition with the hips.

Problem 5. Lack of Strength or Flexibility
Sometimes in golf the player is asked to execute a movement he simply isn't capable of performing. For instance, a short, barrel-chested golfer who weighs in the vicinity of 250 pounds will find it impossible to perform a 90-degree shoulder turn. Likewise, a tall, spindly built golfer who weighs less than 100 pounds will find it impossible to control the clubhead during the swing.

The final problem we commonly experience in teaching the transition move resembles this inherent dilemma. Executing the transition move requires some degree of strength and flexibility. To shift your hips vigorously to the left while continuing to turn your upper body in the opposite direction requires suppleness in your trunk region. And to make the transition move really dynamic, you need enough strength in your shoulders, arms, and hands to swing the club down with all the speed and power that the legs and trunk have produced.

If you find yourself having a great deal of difficulty performing the three transition drills, it may be that lack of strength or suppleness is a glaring problem. The good news is that, regardless of the problem, it can be improved or eliminated entirely. Unlike many sports, golf does not take a great deal of strength or flexibility. The bad news is that if you lack the necessary amount of either, it will affect your game dramatically.

The key to success in overcoming strength or flexibility problems lies in the "Weighted Club Transition" drill. If used properly, and often, it will improve both your strength and suppleness.

EVALUATE YOUR PROGRESS

The transition move ends when you have reached the top of the swing. As you'll see in the next chapter, the correct position at the top gives you the opportunity to easily evaluate how well you have prepared for the all-important move to impact.

Chapter Five

Top of the Swing

POISED FOR PERFECTION

The top of the backswing, like the setup, is a position rather than a movement. Perhaps that explains why it receives more attention from pros and amateurs alike than any other stage of the swing. On practice ranges everywhere, you see players freezing their position at the top, then craning their necks to inspect the position of their arms, hands, clubface, and shaft. The urge to check how your swing is coming along at the midway point is powerful, and the momentary lull that occurs when the club has traveled its maximum distance away from the ball provides a ripe opportunity.

The top-of-swing position is widely regarded as the initial determinant of a great downswing. Producing a solid position at the top does give you the ability to produce a successful downswing more effectively, but there is a reason you may play poorly despite arriving at the top in textbook-perfect fashion.

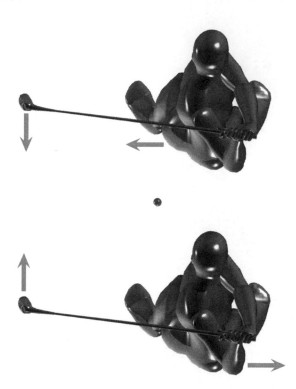

FIG. 5-1. Although both swing positions appear to be perfect, the movement directions make all the difference. The Pro (top) is producing a model swing by moving his hips toward the target, and allowing the clubhead to fall away from the target line (inside path). The impostor (bottom) is creating a high handicap swing by allowing the hips to continue to sway to the right, and moving the clubhead toward the target line (over-the-top).

First, you should understand that the position you achieve at the top is only half the equation. It's important to remember that all the club and body parts must also be moving in the proper direction (fig. 5-1). For example, as the club reaches the top, the hips are already moving toward impact. At the same time, although the clubhead has finally stopped moving back, it continues to move behind you, away from the target line. A snapshot taken at the top cannot reveal this information, since a photograph freezes all movement. The picture of a golfer moving the hips and the clubhead in the wrong directions would look the same, even though the swing results would be radically different.

This word of caution should not detract from the importance of the effort made to arrive at the top in great position. The more correct motions made during the move to the top, the greater the chance you will arrive matching both position and direction as you begin the downswing. Your position at the top has a significant influence on the success of your swing, and understanding its relationship with the downswing is a great step toward achieving lasting improvement. A sound position at the top helps ensure good balance and the right sequence of movement on the downswing. Setting the club in the correct position makes it effectively lighter, so you can swing it down with maximum speed and control along the ideal swing path.

A solid position at the top also helps perpetuate the smooth tempo you established early in the backswing and ultimately leads to a well-timed delivery of the clubhead through impact. Add the proper movement *direction* to this solid position and the downswing becomes a much easier task. In fact, the correct position and direction at the top allows the club to "tell" you how to perform the downswing.

Recognizing the importance of both position and direction, let us discuss what is truly important at the top of the swing.

Many important features of a great top-of-swing position are overlooked because players usually examine details that have a minor bearing, or no bearing at all, on the downswing. For example, amateurs tend to be overconcerned about whether their clubshaft reaches parallel at the top, when physical limitations may make it harmful even to try to attain that position. Meanwhile, they ignore completely an extremely critical factor such as knee flex, which has the potential to ruin any possibility of performing the downswing correctly. A poor understanding of cause and effect in the swing sets them on the road to ruin even before they begin to move the club forward.

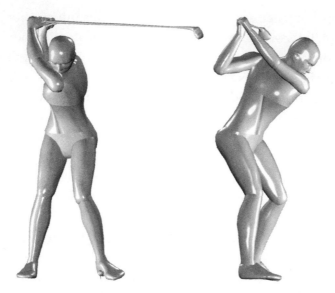

FIG. 5-2. The model top-of-swing position. The face-on view (left) shows the Pro moving the lower body toward impact as the club finishes its backward path. The down-the-line view (right) shows the coiled body position, ready to begin the powerful unwinding action.

First and foremost, the top of the swing should be used as a tool to determine how well you have performed the grip, setup, backswing, and transition components. If those aspects of the swing are sound, you should arrive at the top in a good position naturally, without having to adjust or manipulate your body or the club (fig. 5-2). If you have a flaw early on, it probably will manifest itself in some way when you reach the top.

Beyond that, there are only a few features we feel deserve constant attention and maintenance. Get them right and you'll set the stage beautifully for a perfect downswing. This is one of the easiest stages of the swing to work on because, for a brief moment, your body movements are minimal. You can easily discern what is happening with the club and your anatomy.

FIG. 5-3. The Pro produces the squat by moving the right hip away from the target line, maintaining the flex in the right knee, and shifting the weight toward the right heel.

IMPORTANCE OF THE "SQUAT"

The most salient feature among good players at the top of the swing (and clearly the most overlooked) is a position we have termed the "squat" (fig. 5-3). Viewed from down the target line, the body weight has shifted rearward toward the right heel, while both knees maintain about the same degree of flex as at address. How does this happen? As your right hip rotates behind you on the backswing, and carries your lower trunk and right leg along with it, the lion's share of your weight naturally accompanies it and winds up primarily on your right heel. This is a sign of a full, correct turn.

When performed properly, our students tell us that it feels like squatting down into a chair. Since the natural tendency is to raise the

FIG. 5-4. Whether it be golf, tennis, or baseball, the squat allows the player to move toward impact in a powerful position.

body at the top, a concerted effort is required to keep the body down. In fact, this is one of the most common errors in the golf swing. It is also an error that we call accumulative since it guarantees that another error must be made later in the swing to correct the unwanted body movement. In this case, raising the body at the top of the swing forces the golfer to drop the body back down during the downswing simply to make contact with the ball. Hitting a small ball with a long club that is moving at 100 miles per hour is difficult enough without moving your eyes up and down.

The squat does much more than simply hold the head steady during the swing. Keeping the body down and coiled places you in a strong athletic position. This squatted position, seen in all sports where explosive body action is involved, stretches the powerful leg and trunk muscles in preparation for moving the body with strength and control (fig. 5-4).

MAINTAINING YOUR BALANCE

Perhaps the most difficult balancing act in golf is the fine line found at the top of the swing (fig. 5-5). With the majority of the weight on the right side, and the hips and shoulders turned away from the target, you must have precise control of your balance if you are going to get back to the ball at impact.

The key to balance at the top is the transition. As the lower body

FIG. 5-5. At the top, the Pro is precariously balanced over the right leg. Only the proper transition move allows him to move to his left during the downswing.

FIG. 5-6. As the clubhead finishes its backward movement, the Pro has used the transition to load and stretch the trunk muscles. Like powerful rubber bands, these large muscles will supply most of the power in the downswing.

begins moving toward the target, the upper body and arms must continue to move and turn away from the ball (fig. 5-6). The result is a balanced body position at the top.

The transition also controls the amount of body rotation. As the hips begin rotating back toward the target, they begin stretching the trunk muscles that connect the hips and shoulders. This not only helps to stop the shoulders from rotating but also stretches and winds the trunk into a very powerful position.

This has been described using many terms, including the "stretch," the "load," and the "X-factor," but whatever it is called, the result is explosive power. It shouldn't come as a surprise that players who best use this loading action are also the ones hitting the ball the greatest distances.

FIG. 5-7. Even though the Pro crosses the line slightly with the driver (left), and is minimally laid off with the 9-iron (right), the goal should be to point the club at the target.

CLUB ALIGNMENT IS THE KEY

It's only natural to want to observe your body positions at the top of the swing. But remember: the purpose of correct body movement is to ensure that the *club*—the only thing that contacts the golf ball—is moved and positioned correctly. The position of the club at the top is critical, and fortunately it's easy to monitor because the club momentarily comes to an almost complete halt.

At the top, the shaft of the club should be aligned directly at your target. Actually, the position varies slightly depending on the club you are using, but that's the basic point of reference from which you should never deviate (fig. 5-7). With the driver, the club actually moves "across the line," or points slightly to the right of the target, at the top. With the short irons, the clubshaft is slightly "laid off," or aimed slightly to the left of the target.

Much has been made of this apparent difference between the long and short clubs, implying a difference in the type of swing you make for each. In fact, if you consider the length of the club you are using and the accompanying length of swing, the swing paths of all clubs are the same (fig. 5-8). The length of the driver, and your objective of hitting the ball as far as possible, produces a longer swing and a flatter swing path. In contrast, the accuracy demands of the much shorter 9-iron results in a more up-right, abbreviated swing. But if the shape of each swing path is examined, the swing paths for both clubs, and for all those in between, are strikingly similar.

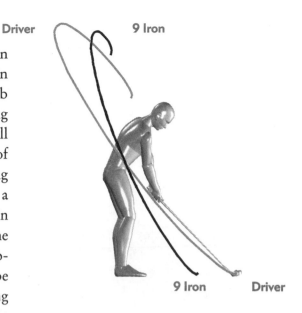

FIG. 5-8. Although the backswing path of the driver (blue) is flatter than the 9-iron (black), the shape of the paths are almost identical.

LET THE CLUB DO THE WORK

Although most of the emphasis is placed on position at the top of the swing, the factor that makes the most difference is virtually impossible to see. That factor is the quality of the transition and how it causes your body and the club to move. The transition is so dramatic—and so subtle—that two golfers can reach identical positions at the top and yet maintain handicaps that are 36 strokes apart.

We have placed great emphasis on the importance of the transition in leading the downswing and producing power. Getting the lower body moving first has several other effects that begin to show up at the top of the swing. The most obvious benefit is that, by leading with the hips, the lower body is moved out of the way, allowing the arms and club to travel along an inside path en route to the ball. To accomplish this, however, the hips must be moving forward at the top of the swing. Delaying this movement or, more disastrously, moving the hips away from the target at the top will throw the entire swing out of sync.

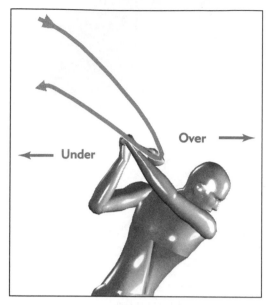

FIG. 5-9. Producing the proper movements to the top of the swing allows the Pro to drop the club under as the downswing begins.

Even more important, however, the proper transition allows the club to move correctly and helps you produce a solid downswing. Many players comment that, when they are swinging well, they feel that they are just "getting out of the way" of the clubhead. They are swinging the club so well that they would actually have to make a concerted effort to disrupt the path their club is following naturally.

Scientists use the term "inertia," while golfers refer to "dropping the club under." Whatever your preference, it is critical that you route the clubhead on an inside path during the downswing. The potential success of this effort can be seen at the top. If everything has been properly prepared, the clubhead is actually moving backward, away from the target line, at the top of the swing (fig. 5-9). If you can get the clubhead moving in this direction, it is impossible to avoid swinging on an inside path during the downswing. Likewise, if your clubhead is moving in the opposite direction, you cannot help but produce the dreaded, outside-to-inside, over-the-top, slice-producing downswing path.

There is no magical way to produce this club movement. It is simply your reward for starting with a good setup, followed by a solid backswing and transition.

USING THE TOP AS A BENCHMARK

The reason teachers and players use the top of the swing as a reference point is that the lack of motion makes it easier to feel, sense, and see what is happening with your swing mechanics. Precise determinations of position, sequence of movement, and other details are extremely difficult to discern when your body is going full blast during other stages of the swing. You are looking at the ball, not your body, so there are no visual clues as to what is happening. You are preoccupied only with striking the ball and therefore can't direct attention to some distant point of your anatomy. Drills are always helpful, which is why we emphasize them so strongly throughout this book. But the game would be much easier to teach if the swing didn't entail so much motion.

THE TOP-OF-SWING DRILLS

The first five top-of-swing drills aren't really drills in the classic sense. Rather, they are position checks that will reveal whether you have swung the club to the top with your body and the club in a sound manner. Practice them often and blend them into the work you perform on other segments of the swing. They'll go a long way in helping you tie the whole model swing package together. The final drill is a classic motion drill, and you may well find that it dramatically changes your golf game.

If you have difficulty turning your head to observe your position when the club is swung all the way to the top, have a friend give you an assist. An extra pair of eyes is always helpful.

1. Master the Squat

Because the squat position is the most overlooked component of a correct top-of-swing position, you'll want to practice this drill often. When you master the drill and apply it to your swing, you'll quickly know why the position is called the squat. If done properly, it guarantees three great actions:

Action 1 The head and upper body move down slightly.
Action 2 Your right hip and buttocks rotate to your rear.
Action 3 Your weight shifts to your right heel.

For this drill, you will need the teaching shaft described in the Teaching Introduction. Place the shaft in the ground, 6 inches directly in back of your right heel.

FIG. 5-10. Begin by placing the teaching shaft six inches in back of your right heel.

At address, the shaft will be several inches to the rear of your right hip (fig. 5-10). Now swing to the top and hold your position. Your goal is to touch the shaft with your right hip (fig. 5-11). To accomplish this, the right leg must maintain the same degree of flex as at address. If it straightens, you won't shift your weight to your right heel and your hip won't reach the teaching shaft.

Because your body probably isn't accustomed to making such a dynamic movement, you may lose your balance at first. Make several practice swings, holding the position until you can balance yourself properly. Study the sensation and commit it to memory.

This is one drill you should incorporate into your actual swing as soon as possible. Once you feel comfortable performing it, try

FIG. 5-11. Swing to the top, touching the shaft with your right hip while maintaining flex in your right leg. Satisfying those two objectives results in a full, powerful turn.

hitting some balls with the shaft in place, checking only that your right hip is making contact with the shaft. At the top, the sensation should be one of the body actually squatting down. You should feel primed and ready to move your left side out of the way on the downswing while your right side moves down and under through impact.

You may have experienced the unique feeling of the squat before. Many of our students associate the sensation with those experienced in other sports—a tennis player hitting a forehand shot, for instance, or a baseball player getting into position to swing the bat forward with enough force to hit a home run. In both of those cases, the athlete lowers onto his right side so as to prepare his body for a powerful forward thrust when he strikes the ball.

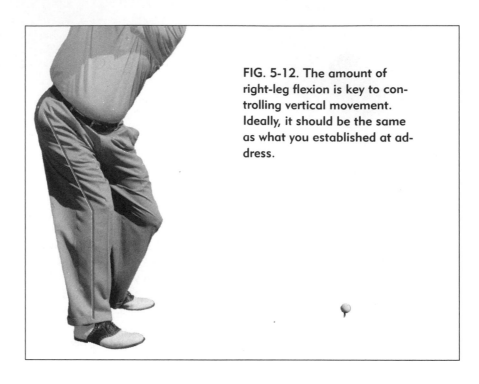

FIG. 5-12. The amount of right-leg flexion is key to controlling vertical movement. Ideally, it should be the same as what you established at address.

2. Right-Leg Flexion

In order for your weight to transfer back to your right heel and for your upper body to lower slightly as it should, you must maintain the same degree of flex in your right knee as you established at address. To perform this drill, swing to the top, stop, and check that your knee flex hasn't increased or decreased (fig. 5-12). After several swing checks, make a full swing, feeling the same flexion at the top of the swing.

The most common error is to straighten the right leg as the club travels vertically on its journey to the top. It's a serious mistake. Straightening the right leg prompts you to raise your trunk at the same time, making your entire posture much too vertical. Once this mistake is made, you are forced to "go down after it" during the downswing, and striking the ball consistently becomes all but impossible.

3. Align the Tee

As we stated, the clubshaft must not be aligned to either the extreme left or the extreme right of the target at the top. Because it can be difficult to tell exactly where the shaft is aligned from your perspective looking upward and in back of you, a great shortcut is to place a tee in the butt of the club and observe where it is pointing at the top of the swing (fig. 5-13). The precise direction the tee points depends on the club you are using, but it should be aimed roughly down your target line. Once you feel comfortable with the club position, hit the ball while envisioning the same tee alignment at the top.

The tee is a useful indicator of the proper club position, but don't rely on it exclusively. For precision's sake, have a friend tell you where your club is aligned at the top.

4. Match the Shaft

Like the preceding drill, this check will enhance your ability to sense where the club is aligned at the top. Place a club on the ground, 6 inches in front of your toes, aimed dead at the target. Merely swing your club to the top and, noting the position of the club on the ground, try to set the club you are using parallel to the club laid along your feet (fig. 5-14).

Have a friend tell you when the two clubs are exactly parallel, and commit the sensation to memory as best you can. Repeat the drill often until you can align the club perfectly without having to inspect its position. As you become more skilled at swinging the club

Target

FIG. 5-13. A hole in the bottom of your grip will accommodate a tee (top). At the top of the swing, the tee should point directly down your target line (bottom).

FIG. 5-14. A good top-of-swing check is to align the club you are holding with a club on the ground set parallel to the target line.

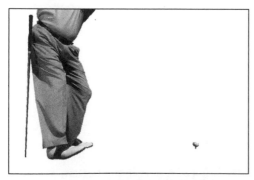

FIG. 5-15. If you are balanced at the top of the swing, you'll be able to lift the toe of your right foot off the ground, and hold it in place.

back so it is aligned properly, hit some balls, remaining conscious of the feeling of the club being in the right "slot" at the top.

5. Toes Up, Knee Inside

At the top, the trick is to get the weight on your right side but retain the ability to get back to the ball. This capability is set up in the transition, but you can check your progress at the top.

Swing the club to the top and stop. If you are balanced correctly, you should be able to lift your right toes with little effort (fig. 5-15). If you have difficulty, place the teaching shaft in the same position used in the "Master the Squat" drill to help get your right side back.

At the same time, if you look down at your right leg, your knee should be inside (toward the target side) of your right foot.

After several dry runs to the top, hit a ball with the same position goals in mind.

6. Drop It Under

If you are tired of your slice and have never brought the club down on an inside path, this drill is for you. Begin by swinging back, stopping the club when it reaches the end of the backswing (fig. 5-16). Before continuing, check that your hips and shoulders are turned properly and your weight is on your right foot. Finally, from the down-the-target-line view, your hands should be inside your shoulder and the club should be aligned perpendicular to the ground.

Begin the drill by completing the swing to the top. As the hands and club move back, shift

FIG. 5-16. The first step of the Drop It Under drill is to swing the club back until it is vertical to the ground.

FIG. 5-17. When you perform the transition and move into the downswing, the clubshaft should flatten so it is no longer vertical. This is the key to producing a correct inside swing path.

and turn your hips toward the target. When the club begins to move, focus on allowing the clubhead to fall away from the target line (fig. 5-17). Initially, do the drill slowly, stopping your swing as the club comes back to the starting position. Check that the clubhead has, in fact, dropped behind the beginning position.

After you get comfortable with this movement, try hitting the ball. The presence of the ball will dramatically increase the difficulty of completing this drill successfully. If you typically slice the ball, you will find it very awkward to even make contact. This shouldn't surprise you, since you are trying to produce a path that is exactly opposite from the one that is normal to you. Keep at it, however, and you will find yourself hitting draws for the first time in your life.

ERRORS TO FILL A LESSON BOOK

The consequences of a poor position at the top are always the same: you can't help but make a poor movement (or a series of them) to achieve contact with the ball. There are a host of errors golfers make at the top of the swing, and they all are insidious, creeping up on you and causing problems without your knowing what exactly went wrong. Errors at this stage of the swing have kept the lesson books of teaching professionals full for ages.

COMMON TOP-OF-SWING PROBLEMS

Of the errors you can commit at the top, four rate as true swing killers. Fortunately, the ability to stop and check the swing at the top makes attacking these problems much easier.

Problem 1. Raising Up During Backswing

This is not a top-of-swing problem per se, since it begins midway into the backswing. But its effect on the top-of-swing position is readily apparent (fig. 5-18), and it destroys your ability to generate maximum power with consistency. It requires that you lower your body on the downswing as much as you raised it on the backswing, and doing that precisely while the club is traveling at high speed is a task beyond the grasp of mere mortals.

The formula for raising up at the top of the swing includes straightening the right leg, moving out on your toes, and straightening your upper body. The cure is to use the "Master the Squat" and "Right-Leg Flexion" drills to make the squat a permanent part of your swing.

Problem 2. Club Crosses the Line

Another serious problem is allowing the club to drift toward the target line at the top of the swing so it "crosses the line"

FIG. 5-18. The student's posture at address is sound enough (left), but he raises his entire body during the backswing (right). This forces him to drop the same amount during the downswing, making impact a hit-or-miss proposition.

and points too far to the right (fig. 5-19). There are many ways to produce this position, but primarily it is caused by faulty manipulation of the arms or wrists during the move to the top. Regardless of the cause, the result is that the clubhead is moving in the wrong direction, ensuring a downswing that will be, at best, too vertical.

If you cross the line and perform the transition move properly, your clubhead will recover and follow an acceptable path. Unfortunately, your angle of approach will be too steep, or vertical, resulting in pulled shots to the left, snap hooks, or some combination of the two.

FIG. 5-19. The Pro reaches the top of the swing with the club pointing toward the target (left). If the club crosses the line (right), the downswing movements that result will produce severe ball flight problems.

If you cross the line and fail to perform the transition, the clubhead will continue on its outward, over-the-top path, resulting in a roundhouse slice.

If you fall in this category, the "Align the Tee," "Match the Shaft," and "Drop It Under" drills are designed for you.

Problem 3. Poor Base of Support

There are a number of ways to cancel out or simply fail to use the power your body is capable of supplying to your golf swing. As it applies to the top of the backswing, the most devas-

FIG. 5-20. The Pro has most of the weight on the right side at the top, but maintains balance and control (left). The student (right) has shifted his weight too far to the right, outside his base of support. From this position, it's doubtful he'll be able to shift the lower body back to the left.

tating power loss occurs when you allow your body to drift laterally outside your base of support (fig. 5-20). Your weight should *never* be shifted so far to the right that you are on the outside of your right foot. When that happens, you will lose your balance and find it impossible to shift your weight back to your left side as you move into the downswing.

The primary cause of excessive lateral movement at the top is poor execution of the transition. Practicing the "Toes Up, Knee Inside" drill and reviewing the Transition chapter will remedy this error.

FIG. 5-21. A full turn is essential, and the Pro uses the hip and shoulder turn to load the powerful trunk muscles (left). The student demonstrates that it's possible to turn to excess (right). This much rotation actually diminishes power instead of creating it.

Problem 4. Loose, Excessive Body Turn

The final swing killer that is apparent at the top of the swing involves too much body rotation (fig. 5-21). Although many golfers fail to turn the body enough on the backswing, turning excessively is every bit as disastrous. The transition move and change of direction with the upper body occur quickly, and your body must be in position to respond. When you turn your hips and shoulders too far, they cannot recover in time to deliver the club to impact in a sound position.

As is the case with shifting your body laterally to an extreme, turning too much is a problem almost exclusively related to a late or nonexistent transition. The shifting and turning of the hips back to the left at the proper time tends to restrict the backswing turn just enough to keep you in balance and in proper position to begin a successful downswing.

As with the problem of excessive shifting, the "Toes Up, Knee Inside" drill and a review of the Transition chapter will remedy this error.

HEADING TOWARD IMPACT

If the amount of material we've presented to this point seems exhaustive, take heart. Impact, the moment when you can reap the rewards for all your hard work, is only ¼ second away—at least in terms of the time it takes to deliver the clubhead to the ball from the top of the swing. Of course, there is the matter of the downswing, which we'll discuss in the next chapter. Your swing is very near the payoff point, so hang in there.

Chapter Six

Downswing

ACHIEVING DISTANCE WITH ACCURACY

Many factors contribute to the makeup of a world-class golfer. He has the ability to control his emotions: to concentrate despite distractions, to stay calm under pressure, to accept bad breaks, and to discipline himself always to play within his capabilities. Intelligence is important, too; he knows when to gamble and when to play it safe, how to formulate a strategy and how to stick to it. Physical conditioning is also a factor; the golfer who possesses strength, flexibility, and stamina enjoys a considerable advantage over his flabby opponent. Determination, competitiveness, experience—the list of attributes goes on and on.

In the end, however, all of those factors take a backseat to the fundamental challenge of hitting the ball with both power and precision. Developing a swing that produces a superb blend of distance and accuracy is what the game is all about. Every real golfer knows this, and the end-

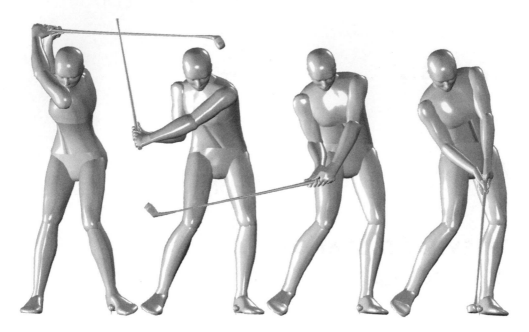

FIG. 6-1. The downswing in golf is one of the most explosive movements in sport.

less hours spent refining the swing, taking lessons, shopping for the latest in top-of-the-line equipment, reading instruction books, watching videotapes, playing, and even thinking about golf bears this out.

So which stage of the swing is the most prominent determinant of distance and accuracy? If you were to put the issue to a vote, the winner, hands down, would be the downswing (fig. 6-1). There is an instinctive sense that the most decisive moment of the swing occurs as the body and club move fast and furious toward the ball, the thrill of impact a fraction of a second away. It is the most ephemeral stage of the swing and is perceived as the most difficult to work on since everything happens so quickly and automatically that errors are difficult to detect. The suspicion remains that the elusive blend of distance and accuracy is buried deep within the mysterious movements of the downswing.

Historically, the quest to become "long and straight" has been viewed as a question of "Which do you want?" The average golfer has been schooled to believe that the swing movements that produce distance tend to diminish the ability to hit the ball straight. A John Daly–like backswing, with the enormous shoulder turn that transports the club well past parallel at the top, can produce prodigious distance but is not conducive to pinpoint precision. Conversely, a shorter, more controlled swing may produce string-straight drives, but the smaller range of motion limits the ability to generate the clubhead speed necessary to launch the ball into the stratosphere.

So which will it be? For the average golfer, there is heartening news. *Unless you can drive the ball 250 yards consistently (220 yards for a woman), eliminating the flaws in your swing will improve both distance and accuracy.* That's because the factors that cost you power and control are not the result of poor strength and flexibility but of errors that occur during the swing. For the overwhelming majority of amateurs, the distance/accuracy "trade-off" is an illusion. By eliminating swing mistakes and making your motion more efficient, you'll enjoy the maximum distance you're capable of achieving and hit the ball straighter as well.

No doubt about it, the distance/accuracy trade-off is rooted in truth. But it is a good player's dilemma. Justin Leonard, the 1997 British Open champion, is a fairly short hitter by tour standards (he averages about 260 yards with his driver). Yet he is also incredibly accurate. Leonard probably could increase his distance by lengthening his swing or simply applying more reckless power on the downswing, but he would do so at the expense of his amazing accuracy. He rides a very fine line. Is the sacrifice in accuracy worth 10 more yards? Probably not.

The average golfer, on the other hand, is neither as long as Leonard nor as straight, even though Leonard stands only about 5 feet 8 inches tall and weighs 150 pounds. The source of the everyday player's lack of distance and accuracy obviously is poor swing mechanics, many of which occur during the downswing. For him, increased distance is not necessarily a matter of lengthening the swing but of performing the downswing gracefully with all the body parts moving in proper sequence. The same is true of accuracy. He needn't shorten his swing impulsively but rather should streamline his movements so the clubface is delivered back to the ball along the proper path and in a perfectly square position.

From a standpoint of fast, dynamic movement, the downswing is definitely where the action is. That is what we'll teach and discuss in this chapter: the movements that will guarantee plenty of distance with a potential gain, not loss of accuracy. It is a worthwhile, attainable goal for virtually every amateur golfer.

A DOWNSWING PREFACE

In developing golfers, there are a number of improper swing actions that decrease both distance and accuracy in the downswing. They can basically be divided into two categories (fig. 6-2):

Category 1 Those that occur before you reach the top of the swing.

Category 2 Those that occur after the downswing has begun.

It is important that you trace your problem to the correct source.

If your swing is either short and/or crooked, look first to Category 1. By a huge margin, the problems typically experienced during the downswing are caused by problems that occur much earlier. Many players work extremely hard to improve the downswing motion when, in fact, the problem doesn't lie there at all. By performing the setup, grip, backswing, transition, or top-of-swing poorly, your fine execution of the forward swing will be totally ineffective. Regardless of your timing, strength, or athleticism, you are rendered helpless by the poor positions and movements that preceded it.

Review the material we've recommended to this point. Make sure

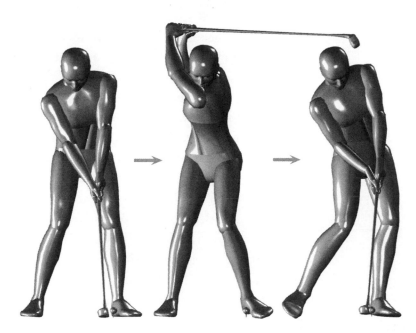

FIG. 6-2. Most of the problems in a swing are caused by errors made during the swing to the top (left to middle). Begin to look for problems in the downswing (middle to right) only when all prior parts are acceptable.

you have the drills down pat. If you are performing them correctly, you can feel confident your problems rest in Category 2—an inefficient downswing in which the club is delivered to impact with neither power nor precision.

DISTANCE: A VIEW TO A THRILL

There are two major downswing components that determine how far you hit the ball. One is related to how you use the powerful muscles of your body; the other is associated with how you position the club.

Right Side Dominates Downswing

Some of the movements you perform during the swing are designed to produce clubhead speed, power, and distance. Other movements are

FIG. 6-3. The keys to distance can be seen best in the face-on view.

FIG. 6-4. The Pro moves the right side strongly into the downswing, dropping the right elbow (blue) under the left arm.

geared to produce accuracy and control. The two sets of motions, though closely interrelated, are distinct from one another and are readily apparent when viewed from specific perspectives.

The chief producers of *distance* are best viewed from the face-on view (fig. 6-3). If you want more yards with all your clubs, you want to study the swing from this perspective and emulate the movements performed by the best in the game.

Study in particular the cooperative movement between the lower and upper body in the early stages of the downswing. When you perform the transition move, the lower body (the hips and legs) moves emphatically toward the target, your weight beginning to shift from your right side to your left. The combination of lateral and rotary motion in your hips doesn't release all the power in your swing just yet; rather, it continues to accumulate as your upper body keeps turning to the top of the swing.

As the downswing begins, an amazing sequence of events takes place. The enormous amount of elastic energy accumulated in the muscles of your torso gradually begins to release. Your upper body follows the lead established by your lower body, unwinding as your weight continues to shift from your right side to your left. The focal point of your upper body movement is the right shoulder. It moves down and forward as the upper portion of your right arm moves closer to your right side. The emphatic movement of the right side is apparent in that you can see the right elbow dipping lower than the left arm well before your hands reach hip height on the downswing (fig. 6-4).

As the downswing progresses, the co-ordinated movement between the lower and upper body results in tremendous speed and power applied to your club and, ultimately, the ball. But success in the downswing is due to more than just raw strength. By performing the targetward move with the lower body correctly, the upper body can then move in a mechanically efficient manner so no power is wasted. Every ounce of energy is poured into the swing, with none of it squandered through disjointed or awkward movements. The power comes not just through strength, but through proper use of physics.

As important as the act of producing power is the ability to direct it properly.

FIG. 6-5. Even with a model transition, the Pro has just enough room to clear the right arm (blue) during the downswing.

By driving the lower body toward the target, you move the hips out of the way so that the arms can swing on an inside path toward ball contact (fig. 6-5). Our research has shown that the clearance between the arms and the body is so small that, if the lower body is not moved out of the way, the path the arms and club are supposed to follow becomes blocked. The arms are forced to go around the hips, producing an outside-to-inside, over-the-top path that results in a pull and/or slice.

Evidence of the tremendous accumulation of power and its expulsion into the ball can be found in the position of the right foot at the moment the shaft becomes parallel to the ground. Note that only the toe of the right foot is still in contact with the ground. That is proof positive that the weight has been shifted almost entirely from the right side and is now primarily supported by the left leg (fig. 6-6).

At this stage of the downswing, impact is just .03 seconds away. If things aren't right with your swing by now, they never will be. Any correction is humanly impossible.

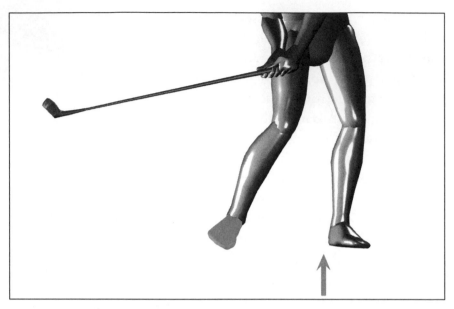

FIG. 6-6. As impact approaches, the body weight (blue arrow) has been shifted so far to the left that the right heel has been pulled off the ground, leaving only the toe of the foot (blue) still in contact.

The Magical Release Angle

A well-known yet somewhat sophisticated term in teaching circles is "retaining the release angle." This expression refers to the angle created by the left arm and the clubshaft during the downswing. It plays a critical role in your ability to generate clubhead speed and greater distance. The basic rule is this: the more acute the angle, and the longer you can retain that angle during the downswing, the farther you will hit the ball.

Most golfers believe that it requires great strength to create a sharp release angle and maintain it deep into the downswing. After all, that's how professional long drivers blast the ball 400 yards or more. But deficiency of strength isn't the chief reason average players lack distance. Rather, it's poor use of the strength they possess, and inadequate setting and releasing of whatever angle they are capable of producing (fig. 6-7).

FIG. 6-7. Good mechanics is the only way to produce a model release angle. It must be allowed to happen, and no amount of effort or determination can force it to occur.

One of the most common sources of power loss is the average players' tendency to "lose" the release angle too early in the downswing. Their clubhead speed is prematurely expended, leaving little left for impact. Moreover, the manner in which they lose the angle not only diminishes clubhead speed but also causes the clubhead to arrive at the ball at a poor angle, resulting in a glancing blow that exacerbates the distance loss.

You needn't create and maintain the release angle like Ben Hogan or Tiger Woods to hit the ball farther. The angle we prescribe for all golfers, which is attainable for anyone with average strength and coordination, is this: the clubshaft and left forearm must form at least a 45-degree angle at the moment the left arm is parallel to the ground. It is worth pointing out that the angle is greatest at this point in the swing. The angle narrows primarily because of the way the lower body and right side work as the move toward the target gets under way.

FIG. 6-8. The criteria for accuracy can best be viewed from down the target line view.

ACCURACY: THE ANGLE ON PRECISION

Although more distance is the goal of most golfers, accuracy really is the key to consistent improvement. If you excel in ball control, any increase in distance will result in an immediate improvement in your scores. Without accuracy, however, the only thing greater distance will get you is deeper in the woods, or an increase in the severity of your slice or hook. Improve your accuracy and game improvement will follow naturally.

Cleared for Approach

The conditions necessary for *accuracy*—a square clubface, the correct swing path, and the most desirable angle of approach of the club-head—are readily apparent when viewing the swing from down the target line. If your shots aren't flying straight, the errors you are mak-

FIG. 6-9. Early in the downswing (left), the hips are already open to (facing) the target, while the shoulders are still well short of their starting position. Just before impact (right), the shoulders still remain closed to the target.

ing will immediately become apparent when comparing your positions to those of the proficient players (fig. 6-8).

The feature most conducive to accurate ball striking is the way the hips shift and rotate, or "clear," on the downswing. Fairly early, well before the angle between the left arm and clubshaft begins to widen as you release the club, the hips have turned so far as to be aligned to the left (open) of the target. They continue to unwind aggressively until the ball is struck. Meanwhile, although the shoulders have rotated downward, they remain aligned to the right (closed) of the target (fig. 6-9).

The open hips/closed shoulders relationship is extremely important in terms of accuracy. When you "clear" your hips in this manner, your shoulders have plenty of room to gather speed and rotate freely through impact. The fact that the shoulders are aligned to the right late in the downswing ensures that the arms and clubhead can approach the ball from inside the target line. A flawless swing path is predestined, and the clubface will be perfectly square at impact, thanks to your model grip. There is no place the ball can go but dead at the target.

Although the right leg maintains the flexion produced by the squat position to keep the right side down, the left leg straightens to help clear the hips. This, combined with keeping your trunk angle virtually constant from setup through impact, guarantees good balance.

Path and Pitch, the Keys to Accuracy

With all the talk of correct body positions and movements, you must remember that it is the clubface that strikes the ball. In fact, the real goal of swinging like the best players in the game is to allow the club to move along the proper path *and* on the correct pitch. This may sound simple, but the dearth of single-digit handicaps points to the difficulty in getting them both right.

Every golfer is familiar with the term "swing plane." Although this concept was debunked in the Introduction, the underlying concept that club movement is important is right on target. Unfortunately, unless you are built like the mechanical Iron Byron, your club will *never* follow the same plane from start to finish. Instead, you will have to deal with the problems of both path and pitch.

When we deal with path of the club, we focus on both the butt end and the head of the club. When these paths are examined in tour players, two features are obvious. First, the downswing paths of both the hands and club are decidedly inside-to-square (fig. 6-10). No surprise there, since this has always been a fixture in everyday teaching.

The surprise lies in the second feature, which is apparent when comparing the clubhead downswing path with the backswing path. Of the more than 100 tour players we analyzed, the downswing paths of all but one of the players were *outside* the paths produced during the backswing (fig. 6-11). This was also true with the hand paths. In golf terminology, the overwhelming majority of the best players in the world are swinging slightly "over the top."

Although the term "pitch" is foreign in golf terminology, the concept is not. Pitch simply refers to the tilt of the club during the swing.

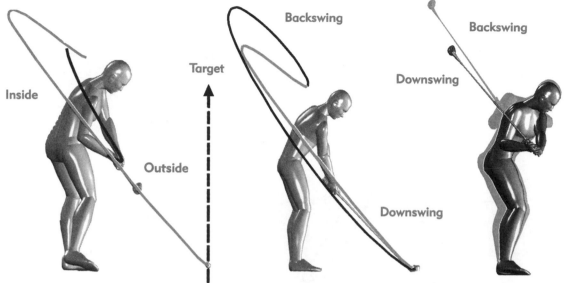

FIG. 6-10. The hand (black) and clubhead paths (blue) of the Pro both move toward the target line (inside-to-square) during the downswing.

FIG. 6-11. Surprisingly, the clubhead downswing path (blue) of the Pro is outside the backswing path (black).

FIG. 6-12. The pitch (tilt) of the clubshaft flattens as the Pro moves from backswing (blue) to downswing (gray).

During the move to the top, the pitch of the club is more toward the vertical. In comparison, the pitch of the club is flatter on the downswing (fig. 6-12).

This change in pitch from the backswing to the downswing has been called many things in golf, from "flattening the shaft" to "laying it on the table." Regardless of your choice of terms, it is a major contributor to a successful golf swing.

Finding the Inside Path

Next to the transition move, keeping the club on the correct path is the most difficult task in golf. Following an inside path is easy on the backswing since the hips and shoulders are turning away from the target. The difficulty comes in keeping the path inside during the transition and downswing, when the hips and shoulders begin rotating toward the target. This is the reason even the best players cannot keep

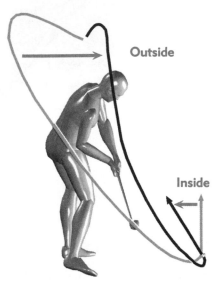

FIG. 6-13. The downswing path of the typical high-handicap student (black) is outside the path of the Pro (blue). The farther away from the model path, the more the swing becomes outside-to-inside or over-the-top.

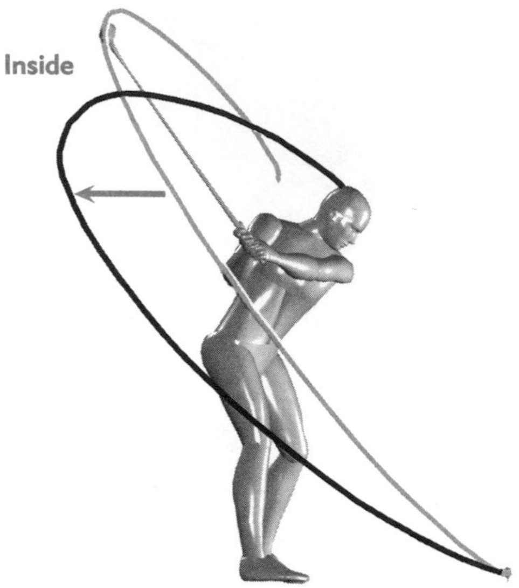

FIG. 6-14. Most developing golfers make the error of swinging the club-head too far inside (black) that of the model path (blue).

their downswing path inside the backswing path. It is also why most developing players trace a path that is too far to the outside (fig. 6-13).

Golf is a game of opposites. Experience has taught us that if a golfer has trouble producing an inside path on the downswing, he will try to fix it by swinging farther inside during the backswing (fig. 6-14). Unfortunately, this invariably throws the club ever farther outside on the downswing.

The only way to produce proper club paths is to reach the top in a good position, then continue the proper body movements in the downswing.

Can You Flatten the Shaft?

Other events transpire as a consequence of fine body movement. As mentioned, on the downswing the clubshaft does not have the same

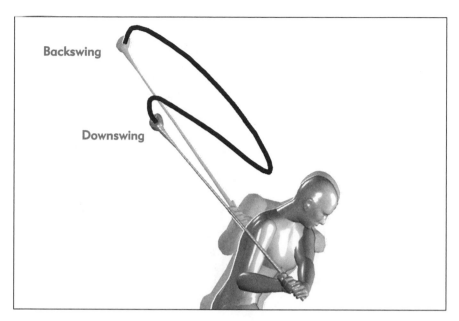

FIG. 6-15. The fall of the club (black path) allows the Pro to flatten the shaft from the backswing (blue) to the downswing (gray).

pitch as it did during the backswing. Because of the "fall" at the top of the swing, the shaft has actually "flattened" compared to the same position on the backswing (fig. 6-15). This flattening of the shaft is common to every good golfer. It ensures that the club will complete its journey to impact efficiently, automatically producing an inside path as well as helping to square the clubface.

Adding to the movements that set up the fall at the top of the swing, the flattening of the shaft is increased due to strong movement of both the lower body and the right side of your upper body. Like so many movements in a model swing, this action of the shaft will occur automatically if your body movements are performed smoothly and correctly.

For a convincing look at this phenomenon, you needn't confine your observations to the images in this book. Turn on your television and

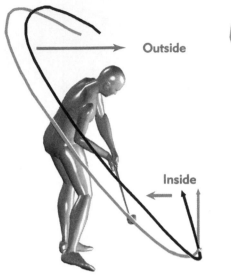

FIG. 6-16. Using the path of the Pro as a reference (blue), the path of the typical golfer is outside during the downswing. This results in an outside-to-inside clubhead movement at impact that results in some combination of pulling and slicing.

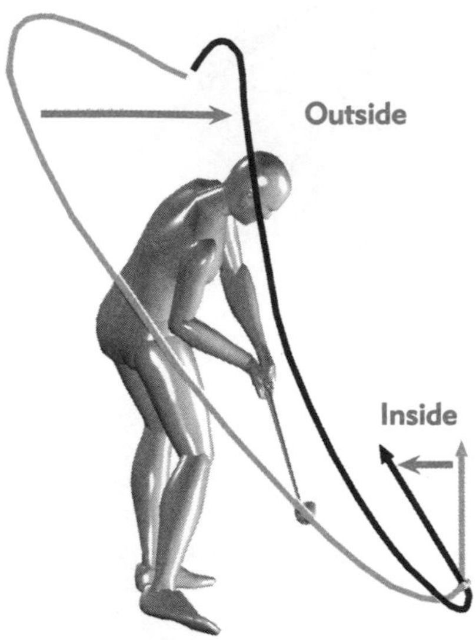

FIG. 6-17. In contrast to the Pro (blue), a downswing path that is outside and steep (black) brings the clubhead severely outside-to-inside, across the ball at impact, creating a major pull-slice. This is the most detrimental path in golf.

watch the best professionals in action. Observe Nick Price in particular; he flattens the shaft more emphatically than any player in golf today.

When Things Go Bad

When problems occur in controlling path and pitch, bad things happen to your ball flight. If your path is outside, putting you in the category of most golfers, you will tend to hit the ball to the left and produce a fade or slice (fig. 6-16).

If you add a steep pitch to the outside path (usually the result of no transition and swinging with the upper body alone), you have the worst combination in golf (fig. 6-17). This will result in a vicious pull-slice.

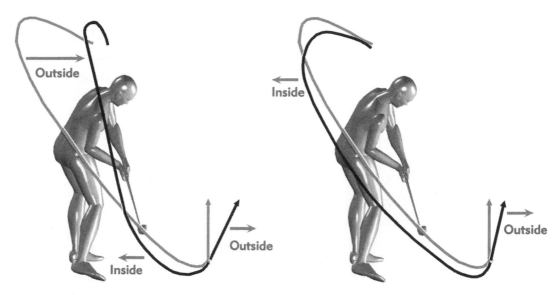

FIG. 6-18. In comparison to the Pro (blue), a downswing path that is initially outside and steep (black) can be brought back inside with a good transition move. This path, created by students moving from high to lower handicaps, can produce hooks that can go in any direction.

FIG. 6-19. A downswing path that matches the Pro (blue), but is too flat (black) brings the clubhead to the ball too far from the inside. This path, produced by many low handicappers, creates a shot that starts to the right and draws back to the middle. If done to excess, it can develop into a major hooking problem.

Golfers making the transition from high handicaps to lower ones commonly combine an outside path with a flat pitch (fig. 6-18). This happens when you don't quite get the body movements correct, but have developed a transition. The result is a shot that may go left or right, but will always hook. If you are a slicer of the ball, this is the pattern you will see on your road to improvement.

The least common path and pitch problem occurs when a golfer has a good path and a pitch that is too flat (fig. 6-19). This is a better player's problem and is produced by a poor clubhead fall at the top of the swing, coupled with an excellent transition and strong move during the downswing. This results in a hook, the pattern most good players fight.

Just Hold On

If everything is done properly, the dynamic lower body and right-side movement instills a "can't miss" quality to the swing as impact approaches. While the left arm remains straight and guides the club into the ball, the right arm remains bent at the elbow and near the torso, ready to unload incredible speed into impact. The right-side movement is so pronounced you can see daylight between the two arms (fig. 6-20). Finally, note that the clubface is slightly closed in relation to the target line. We will explain the importance of this position in the next chapter.

For all purposes, the downswing is complete. From here, all you need to do is relax, hold on, and let the clubhead do the work. A perfect strike is assured.

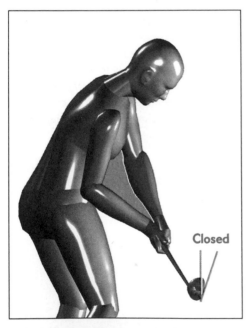

Closed

FIG. 6-20. Daylight between the arms (blue) indicates that the right arm remains flexed and able to provide power as impact approaches. The proper grip also creates a slightly closed clubface angle.

THE DOWNSWING DRILLS

Every one of these drills is designed to encourage you to begin from the correct top-of-swing position, then involve the entire body in the downswing movement. Some of the drills are designed to focus on controlling the large muscles of the body, while others focus on the arms and club. Regardless of the emphasis, these drills are some of the most enjoyable and productive.

1. The Squat, Part II

The first part of the "Master the Squat" drill was presented in the Top of the Swing chapter. Before continuing, you might want to go back for a quick refresher. The goal of that drill was to touch the teaching shaft with your right hip as you arrive at the top of the swing. The following drill begins where that drill left off. The purpose of this expanded drill is to train your lower body

FIG. 6-21. Bump the shaft at the top of the swing (left), then concentrate on moving your hips as fast and full as possible to the left, at the same time moving your right side through the shot (right).

to turn assertively throughout the downswing, so the upper body can follow.

After you swing to the top and touch the shaft with your right hip, move your hip away from the shaft and rotate it toward the target as dramatically and as fast as possible (fig. 6-21). In addition, as part and parcel of the hip movement, try to ingrain the sensation of a "live" right side, your right shoulder moving down and through impact shortly after you begin the hip turn to the left.

Begin the drill without a ball, but make a full swing. When you can feel the power in your right side, begin hitting balls emphasizing the same motion.

FIG. 6-22. Address the ball using your right arm only (left). Make a full, easy swing, stopping at impact (middle). It is imperative that your right hand be farther forward than it was at address, and that your weight be distributed primarily on your left side. Once you satisfy those conditions, hit a series of shots (right), focusing on the correct impact conditions.

2. Right Arm Only

The importance of proper right-side movement can't be emphasized enough. This drill will improve your ability to transport the club downward and forward with your entire right side—hand, arm, and shoulder.

Using your 5-iron, tee a ball fairly low to the ground and hold the club with your right hand only, gripping down so your hand is at the end of the grip just above the shaft. Place your left arm behind your back. Assume your model setup position (fig. 6-22, left), swing to the top, then swing down to impact, stopping when the club draws even with the ball (fig. 6-22, middle). Now check the following positions:

Position 1　Your right hand should be slightly ahead of the ball.

Position 2　Your right heel should be off the ground, your right leg flexed at the knee, your left leg extended.

Position 3　Your hips should be wide open to the target (a 45-degree angle) and your shoulders should be parallel to the target line.

Position 4　The vast majority of your weight—about 90 percent—should be on your left side.

Repeat the drill until you can satisfy all these checkpoints consistently. Take the next step and actually strike the ball (fig. 6-22, right). If done properly, you should be able to hit the ball almost as far as your normal swing.

3. Flatten the Shaft

The flattening of the shaft that occurs on the downswing is not a cause, but an effect. That is to say, if you perform the transition move well and use your lower body correctly, the shaft will flatten as a result. The following drill will indicate the position of the shaft at the same relative positions on the backswing and downswing—and reveal how well you are performing the proper downswing movements.

Using any club, place a tee in the small hole in the butt of the handle. Perform the backswing until the shaft is vertical to the ground from the face-on view, then hold your position. The tee should point to a spot midway between the ball and a line drawn along your toes (fig. 6-23, left).

Continue your swing until the transition move is complete, the downswing has begun, and the shaft has again reached a vertical position. Freeze your body and check again where the tee is point-

FIG. 6-23. When the club reaches the end of the backswing, the butt end of the club should point just inside the ball (left). At the same position in the downswing, the shaft should be flattened sufficiently for the handle to be pointed outside of the ball (right).

ing. If you have flattened the shaft correctly, the tee should aim outside of the ball (fig. 6-23, right).

In addition to refining your downswing, this drill will improve your transition move and ensure that you are swinging the club down along the proper inside path. Repeat it until you get the positions right every time. The next step is to stop in the backswing, check your position, and proceed to strike the ball. Remember to envision the tee pointing outside the ball on the downswing.

4. Sidearm Throw

We've provided several analogies between golf and other sports. This drill likens the correct right-side movement on the down-

FIG. 6-24. The downswing action has been likened to a throw, and these photos show the similarity. The ball is still stationary, yet the lower body is well into the delivery phase (left). In sequence, the shoulders, arm and, finally, the ball follow the lower body into the throw (right).

swing to the throwing motion of a baseball pitcher. It teaches the correct sequence of movement in the downswing, which is very similar to that of the baseball player.

You don't need a club, only a golf ball. Choose a target 20 yards down the practice tee and take your stance the way you would for a normal shot. Now simply throw the ball at the target, using the "sidearm" style in which you whip your arm across your chest (don't throw overhand or in the "submarine" fashion). As you make the throw, take simple note of the following golf swing/baseball throw commonalities:

Commonality 1   Just before you release the ball, notice how your right elbow is ahead of your hand (fig. 6-24, left). The same is

FIG. 6-25. The Pump and Go drill is a great exercise for proper hip shift and turn, and right-side movement. Swing to the top (left), begin the downswing, then

true during the downswing in golf; the powerful right-side movement drives your right elbow down and forward before you release the club into the ball.

Commonality 2   Note how your hips are wide open, facing the target, just as you release the ball (fig. 6-24, right). Your upper body is now joining in and performing its share of the load. This is what happens in golf. The hips "clear out" early in the downswing and rotate until they are aligned open, toward the target. The upper body remains closed until just before impact, then powerfully moves through ball strike.

Once you begin feeling the correct body movements, grab a club and make several practice swings feeling the same actions. Take the final step and begin hitting balls with the same focus.

stop halfway down (middle-left). Repeat this pumping action twice more. On the final effort (middle-right), complete the downswing and strike the ball (right).

5. Pump and Go

This drill fulfills two important goals. First, it improves the "shift-and-turn" action that transpires in your hips and lower body as the downswing commences. Second, it promotes the correct forward and downward movement of your right side early in the downswing. Become proficient at performing this drill and you'll learn to deliver the club into the ball along the correct inside path.

Assume your model setup position. Swing the club to the top of the swing (fig. 6-25, left), perform the transition move, then stop the downswing abruptly when your hands are just above hip level (fig. 6-25, middle-left). Swing the club back up to the top and repeat this downward "pump" move that terminates before you begin to uncock your wrists. On the third go (fig. 6-25, middle-right), let it rip. Hit the ball aggressively (fig. 6-25, right).

FIG. 6-26. By setting up with your feet aligned open to the target, you are forced to swing outside on the backswing (left) and inside on the downswing (right) in order to hit the ball at the target. Notice the full extension of the arms through impact—slicers rarely display this "look."

Remember, you want to pump twice and *then* hit the ball. Be aware of how your right shoulder works downward and your hips rotate open and to the left as you pump the club. Feel the club approaching the ball from inside the target line. This is the feeling you will enjoy when you go back to hitting shots in a normal manner.

6. The Inside Path

If you are an "over-the-top" fader or slicer, this drill will pose a real challenge. Most path drills consist of having golfers radically close their stance and artificially improve their poor path. We have actually analyzed the closed-stance drill and found that, the morale boost it gives to the slicer notwithstanding, it does nothing to improve the swing.

In contrast, the drill we recommend forces an improvement in the club path, or else making ball contact becomes impossible.

Begin the drill by using your 9-iron, selecting a target, and properly addressing the ball. Lay the teaching shaft along your toe line, then simply move your left foot 4 inches away from the ball, producing a stance very open to the target. Begin your backswing by swinging the clubhead to the outside along the open toe line (fig. 6-26, left). From this position, finish the swing, trying to hit the ball at the original target (fig. 6-26, right).

Your initial shots will go to the left, but continued practice will allow you to bring them back to the center. In doing so, you should feel the effort required to keep the club from moving outside the target line on the downswing. At this point, take a normal setup and hit a few with the same motion.

As you become more proficient, you can use longer clubs. We have seen good players—Lee Trevino and Fred Couples are great examples—who are able to hit the driver straight with a stance that is as much as 4 inches open.

COMMON DOWNSWING PROBLEMS

Since the downswing is at the end of the series of swing movements, all your errors will show up here. There is simply not enough space to list every possible problem; however, there are three that dominate the learning landscape.

It is interesting to note that all three problems are related to the lack of proper movement in the lower body and right side. The human body is a miraculous machine, and if you fail to make the right move, it will try to recover the best it can. Unfortunately, if you eliminate the powerful lower body and right side, the only possible compensations available are poor substitutes.

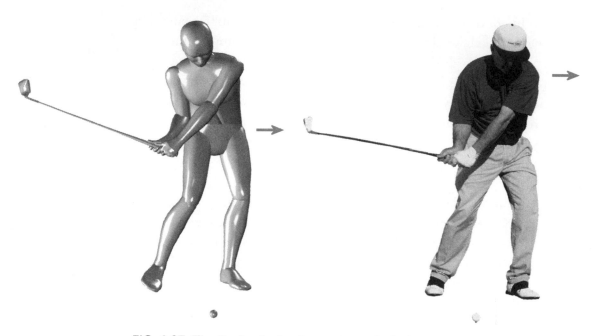

FIG. 6-27. The Pro leads the downswing with the lower body (left). The consequences of an upper-body dive (right) can be seen as the student is forced to release the club too early on the downswing—losing both the power of the lower body as well as the speed of the club.

Problem 1. Upper-Body Dive

If you fail to use your lower body as you should when you move into the ball, the only alternative is to use the *upper* body (fig. 6-27). Initiating the downswing with your upper body prevents you from moving your right side down and through correctly. The result is that you release the club too early, the angle between the left arm and clubshaft widening at the wrong time. The most noticeable consequence is a loss of distance.

Viewing the downswing from down the target line, you can see how the upper-body dive costs you accuracy as well (fig. 6-28). Note how the limited amount of lower-body involvement restricts the hip turn and curbs your ability to channel the club into the ball along the proper swing path. The upper-body dive

FIG. 6-28. The Pro uses the lower body motion to produce the proper down-swing clubhead path (left). Another consequence of the upper-body dive is the unwanted over-the-top path (right). From here, a slice or pull is the only ball flight possible.

is one of the chief causes of the deadly "over-the-top" move, which is tailored perfectly for a nasty pull or slice.

Your top-of-swing position may look like that of a touring pro, but the upper-body dive can instantly transform your swing into that of a hacker. And it only takes the first $\frac{1}{10}$ second of the downswing for it to happen. If this is your problem—and it very well may be—you should review the transition move and make sure your lower body is leading your upper body throughout the downswing. Couple this with work using the "Squat: Part II," "Sidearm Throw," and "Inside Path" drills.

Problem 2. *Weak Right Means Strong Left*

Power loss can be traced to the arms as well as to the body. In fact, the most prominent "power leak" occurs when your right arm lags behind the right side of your torso during the downswing (fig. 6-29). If your right arm doesn't work in concert with the downward movement of your right shoulder, your left arm is forced to dominate the transmission of power. Invariably, you will uncock your wrists too early, costing you all the power you worked so hard to accumulate.

The major reason we advocate a strong right side emphasis is the problems that occur when the right side is a weak contributor. Most of the common problems, from loss of power, to the tendency to slice, to shots that are poorly struck, all are directly related to a weak right side. In all of our teaching experience, we have yet to see a player with too aggressive a right side action.

Use the "Right Arm Only" drill to feel how the right arm works in complete compatibility with the upper right side of the torso. Emulate this position during your downswing and your left-arm dominance problems will cease.

Problem 3. *The "Left-Yank Slice"*

As we intimated in the previous swing problem, left-arm dominance in the downswing is a serious source of weak shots. It is also one of the greatest contributors to the most common ball-flight problem experienced by beginners and veteran hackers alike: the slice. If the left arm leads and is placed in the ill-suited role as dominator, there is no recourse but to throw the clubhead onto the outside-to-inside swing path that produces the slice (fig. 6-30).

In all of our students, from beginners to tour professionals, we have yet to find one who dominates with the left side and is able to successfully play the game.

If you are in this category, the "Flatten the Shaft," "Pump

FIG. 6-29. The Pro uses an active right arm to maintain wrist cock until late in the swing (left). Too much left-side control results in poor positioning and performance with the right arm loss of wrist cock early in the downswing (right).

and Go," and "Inside Path" drills should be a part of every practice session.

THE PAYOFF AWAITS

A sound downswing, combined with proper execution of the earlier fundamentals, guarantees perfect club-ball contact before the moment of truth actually arrives. While that may be so, it doesn't diminish the thrill that awaits when you nail the longest, most accurate shots of your life. In the next chapter, we'll explore the conditions present at the moment of impact and their relation to other components of the swing.

FIG. 6-30. A strong transition and right-side movement lets the clubhead fall backward and produce the desired inside-to-square downswing path (left). If the student pulls down hard with the left arm, with little or no assistance from the right arm, an outside-to-inside swing path (and a slice) is inevitable (right).

Chapter Seven

Impact

THE MOMENT OF TRUTH

Impact is the most dynamic position in golf. Everything you have done to this point has been in preparation for the split second when the clubhead, tearing through the air with incredible speed, compresses the ball and sends it flying off the clubface like a bullet: long, straight, and true. It is at this moment that your entire body, exuding both grace and power, feels the undeniable physical sensation of a purely struck shot vibrating up the clubshaft into your hands. Whether experienced or merely witnessed, this moment is one of the most thrilling in sports.

It has been said that impact is the only position that really matters in the golf swing since it is the only time the club comes in contact with the ball. There's a lot of truth in that. Certainly, if you can produce a picture-perfect impact position, then you are capable of becoming a fine golfer—if you aren't one already. The long list of great players displaying superb impact positions is testament to the fact that it is impossible to be an outstanding ball striker without arriving at the ball in a technically correct, dynamic position.

Impact warrants serious study because it reveals important clues about what transpired earlier in the swing. The soundness of your preswing fundamentals—the grip and setup—are readily apparent when you return the club to the ball. The effectiveness of the backswing and transition, the fullness of the weight transfer, and the sequence of motion they followed on the downswing are reflected by the position of the club and body at impact. The smart swing analyst, like a scientist studying a trail of DNA, can detect swing flaws that occurred early in the swing merely by examining the golfer when ball contact occurs. From that standpoint, impact is a great teaching and learning tool (fig. 7-1).

Yet impact is also beguiling. The revelations of the position alone are definitely limited. For example, a stop-action photograph at impact tells you nothing about the player's clubhead speed or the direction the clubhead is traveling (fig. 7-2). Is the clubhead moving down the target line (a straight shot), inside-to-outside (draw or hook), or outside-to-inside (fade or slice)? These are factors a static view of impact does not reveal.

For all of the variations we've seen in world-class players through the years, the characteristics of impact are the same. The players take slightly different routes to get there, but to obtain the quality impact position that sends the ball flying far and straight, certain conditions must be produced. This is not to say the "route" doesn't matter. To eliminate ungainly midswing corrections that threaten consistency and to be able to arrive at impact naturally without conscious effort, we again urge you to follow our program from start to finish, taking no shortcuts along the way.

FIG. 7-1. Impact: The moment of truth in the swing.

FIG. 7-2. Although the impact position can tell a lot about the quality of your swing, it cannot identify the direction your body and club are moving. Although all three models look the same, only the first (left) is producing the proper inside-to-square clubhead path. The other two produce unwanted inside-to-outside (middle) and outside-to-inside (right) paths.

"LOOKS GOOD, GOES BAD"

Just as the impact position doesn't reveal the direction the clubhead is moving, it also fails to explain the body movements that caused the clubhead to travel on its particular path. Many high-handicap players actually look fairly impressive at impact. That was the case with a foreign student who came to us for help with a lifelong swing problem, an over-the-top move that produced a nasty slice. Viewed from the face-on view, his impact position looked fairly sound. Yet his exaggerated left-to-right ball-flight prompted him to shake his head and mutter, "Looks good, goes bad."

His experience points up the importance of knowing the limitations of analyzing the impact position. Still, gaining an understanding of the correct features at this position can prevent many swing problems as well as cure existing ones.

LOWER BODY HOLDS THE KEY

There are hundreds of features of impact you could scrutinize and try to cross-reference with other parts of the swing, but that many aren't necessary. The characteristics that merit close observation are few but critical. The first series occurs in the lower body and indicates how much power has been generated.

First, note the position of the right heel. From the face-on view, it is apparent that the right heel has come well off the ground. Obviously, very little weight remains planted on the right foot; this is evidence of a strong weight shift to the left. In fact, a full 90 percent of the weight is now on the left leg and foot, supporting the delivery of the club to impact (fig. 7-3).

Viewed from down the target line (fig. 7-4), you can also see how the weight shift, along with the raising of the right heel, is evidence of a strong right-side movement during the downswing. If your right heel is still planted on the ground at this point, you can bet that you haven't involved your entire body in the swing and will pay for it in both lost distance and unwanted ball-flight characteristics.

Second, both knees have shifted emphatically toward the target in an effort to drive the lower body through the shot. Note in the down-the-target-line view how the left knee is well inside the right, indicating that the legs have done the good work of rotating the hips into an open position at impact.

The end result of this dynamic movement of the lower body is to place the hips well in front of the upper body, as well as align them wide open to the target.

FIG. 7-3. At impact, virtually all of the Pro's weight has been shifted to the left side.

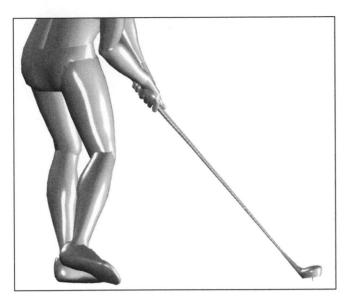

FIG. 7-4. The legs rotate the lower body so aggressively that it pulls the right heel off the ground and produces daylight between the legs.

FIG. 7-5. The powerful move into impact (gray) allows the Pro to move the body well in front of the setup position (blue).

IMPACT IS NOT SETUP

A popular maxim holds that the main goal of impact is to return to the position you established at address. A comparison of the top players at setup and impact exposes that maxim as false. The strong lower body movement toward the target initiated during transition, and continued throughout the downswing, places the hips a full 6 inches ahead of the position they occupied at address (fig. 7-5).

The same movement also brings the hands well forward of their starting position (fig. 7-6), which is why your grip must be slightly stronger than what some teachers consider normal. Moving your hands forward, toward the target, automatically opens the clubface (try it). If you began with a neutral grip and made a perfect swing,

FIG. 7-6. Viewed from above, it is evident that at impact (gray), the hands should be well in front of their setup position (blue).

FIG. 7-7. Only a strong grip allows the Pro to naturally square the clubface as he moves from setup (blue) to impact (gray). Any other grip will force you to manipulate the clubface to control the direction of the shot.

placing your hands 5 inches forward of their starting position, the clubface would be wide open and all your shots would go dead right. Your grip must be strong enough to maintain a perfectly square clubface position at impact.

Now you know why a stronger than neutral grip is used by successful players (fig. 7-7). It is also the reason both the Backswing and Downswing chapters stressed the importance of maintaining a clubface that was slightly closed. It is all done to ensure that the clubface can be delivered in a square position at impact, without having to manipulate the club.

The game of golf can be played with a neutral or a weak grip. In fact, several of the best players in the history of the game, like Hogan and Nicklaus, played with a neutral grip. Like many power players, they used this type of grip to control their tendency to hook the ball. The majority of us don't have this problem and should avoid making things more difficult by using anything but a stronger than neutral grip.

Although the feet, legs, hips, and hands occupy entirely new places at impact, two parts of your anatomy do return to almost the exact positions they were in at address. Your *head* is in exactly the same location (fig. 7-8), which indicates that, as impact approaches, it acts much like an axis around which the rest of your body can shift and turn. Keeping your head as a fairly fixed point during this part of the swing controls the application of power. If your head were to drift to the left along with the movement of your lower body, the amount of dynamic energy you could unleash would be decreased considerably.

The *shoulders* also return to their approximate starting position, although they are tilted under slightly to accommodate the forward position of the hips and hands.

FIG. 7-8. At impact (gray), the head and shoulders should return to the same position they began at setup (blue). The only difference is due to the rotation caused by the Pro moving the rest of the body forward.

The fact that the hips are wide open to the target, while the shoulders are square (fig. 7-9), tells a lot about how a good swing must occur. The aggressive hip shift and turn is used to generate the power in the swing. The shoulders lag behind so that the large trunk muscles can be stretched, then used to accelerate the upper body and club toward impact. At impact, the shoulders are still behind the hips for two major reasons. First, with the hips ahead, they continue to add power and control to the swing since the trunk muscles are still unwinding. Second, to allow the arms to follow an inside path during the downswing, the shoulders must be closed to the target. Only at the instant of contact, when the clubhead is moving directly at the target, should the shoulders return to the square position they were in at setup.

The lesson from the impact-vs.-setup comparison: if you want a powerful golf swing, you must involve the entire body, from setup through impact.

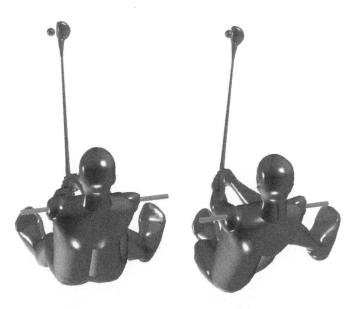

FIG. 7-9. Compared to setup (left), the shoulders should return to virtually the same position at impact (right), even though the hips are wide open to the target.

LOWER BODY CLEARS THE WAY

Focusing on the lower body, it is evident that the superior player is trying to "get out of the way" at the moment of impact (fig. 7-10). The lower body has gone from a square position at address to an open position at impact, the hips aligned well to the left of their starting position. By clearing out the hips, the shoulders and arms have ample freedom to swing to impact and beyond.

The arms continue to function the same as they have throughout the swing. The left is virtually straight at impact, just as it was at every previous stage. The straight position continues to demonstrate its role in guiding the club into the ball along the proper path. The right arm, in contrast, has lost some of the bend it had earlier in the down-

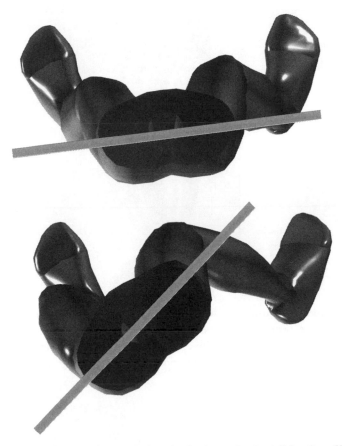

FIG. 7-10. Viewed from above, with only the lower body visible, the effort the Pro makes in getting out of the way as the swing moves from setup (top) to impact (bottom) can be seen. This shift and turn toward the target gives the upper body and arms the room needed to produce an inside path.

swing, but it is still extending and providing power to the swing (fig. 7-11).

There is no more gratifying experience than the feel of the ball moving off the club from a perfect impact position. Once you learn to emulate the proper motion from start to finish, applying all the dynamically perfect ingredients of the model swing, you'll come to expect it every time.

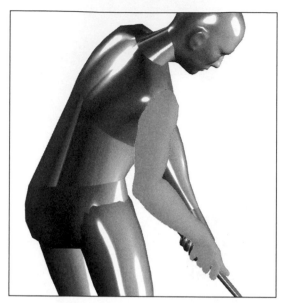

FIG. 7-11. At impact, the Pro continues to use the left arm (gray) as a guide, while extending the right arm (blue) to produce power.

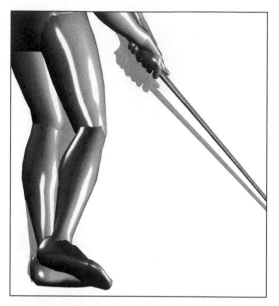

FIG. 7-12. Since centrifugal force drives the hands up from setup (blue) to impact (gray), the clubs must be slightly upright to seat the clubhead flush to the ground.

CLUBS SHOULD BE SLIGHTLY UPRIGHT

We noted in the Setup chapter that the toe of the club should be raised off the turf slightly at address. The upright mode of the clubhead is not done by raising your hands or upper body, but by the specifications of your equipment. All your clubs should be slightly upright.

Here's why: during the late stages of the downswing, centrifugal force tries to pull your left arm and clubshaft into a straight line. This force actually pushes your hands to a higher position at impact than they were at address (fig. 7-12). The act of raising your hands also raises the shaft so that the clubhead, which was set upright at address, is now soled squarely along the turf.

In addition to the higher hand position, the centrifugal force also bends the shaft of the club. This bending, called "droop," drops the clubhead down even more (fig. 7-13). The result is that the lie of the club can change up to 10 degrees from setup to impact. To offset this, your clubs must be upright enough so the toe is actually off the ground at setup. If this is not the case, your toe will be down when impact occurs, which will increase the amount of fade or slice spin placed on the ball. If you are like most golfers, this is the last thing you need.

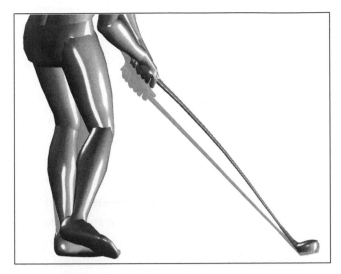

FIG. 7-13. Compared to setup (blue), the forces produced by the Pro at impact (gray) bend the clubshaft downward. To compensate, the clubface angle must be made even more upright.

ALLOWING IMPACT TO HAPPEN

The impact position can't be arrived at consciously. It must be allowed to happen in a free, flowing manner, as a by-product of all the movements and positions that preceded it. The only way this can be achieved is if the proper grip, setup, backswing, transition, top-of-swing, and downswing are produced. We'll drive the point home again: the closer you can come to achieving the model swing positions and movements elsewhere in the swing, the more consistently you will reach the proper impact position.

In interviewing the better players, their overriding feeling as they approached impact was to simply "let it happen." Since better players, as a group, prepare for impact better than their novice counterparts, it's only logical that they believe impact to be primarily a matter of proper preparation.

THE IMPACT DRILLS

The following drills are designed to help you allow impact to occur naturally. To prepare fully and properly, and to ingrain the critical sensations that occur at impact, we've devised three drills that are highly effective at teaching the correct impact position.

1. The Overachiever

As noted earlier, a hallmark of the top player is the ability to shift the body almost completely to the left at impact so that 90 percent of the weight is on the left side and the knees and hips have moved sharply to the left. If you can perfect the following drill, you'll have no problem emulating the model impact position.

On the practice range, place a tee in the ground where you would normally place your ball for a standard 5-iron shot. Three inches in front of the tee, farther up the target line, tee a ball at a height of half an inch. Using your 5-iron, assume your setup position as though you were addressing the first tee, not the ball (fig. 7-14, left).

Now make a normal swing. On the downswing, however, try to move your lower body and right side far enough toward the target to make solid contact with the ball (fig. 7-14, right). Don't be concerned if, at first, you hit behind the ball. That's OK. Keep focusing on moving your lower body forward aggressively until you begin making solid contact. Once you reach this stage, you may find your ball sailing left—way left—of your target. That's OK, too. Solid contact shows you are making progress.

Your next goal, of course, is to straighten out the shot. If you can eventually start the ball to the right of the target and cause it to draw back to the left without losing your balance, you've mastered this move.

This drill forces you to use the lower body and right side to get the hands in front of the ball at impact. If you release the club too soon by not using the lower body or by diving with the upper

FIG. 7-14. In the Overachiever drill, the goal is to position the ball well forward of center at setup (left) and then try to strike it cleanly (right). To be successful, you must shift your weight correctly and emphatically to the left on the downswing.

body, you'll either hit behind the ball, hit the shot to the left, or fail to finish the swing under control.

Remember, think lower body and right side.

2. Clear-Out Drill

This drill also promotes active lower-body movement to the left, so you can free up your right side to make an unencumbered move to impact and beyond. You will need the teaching shaft described in the Teaching Introduction.

To begin, take your setup and place the shaft 5 inches in back and 5 inches to the left of your left heel (fig. 7-15, left). With your 5-iron, make several practice swings, trying to bump the shaft with your

FIG. 7-15. In the Clear Out drill, position the teaching shaft so that you have plenty of room to work the lower body (left). If you can bump the shaft with your left hip prior to impact (right), you've done a great job shifting your weight to the left.

left hip at the moment you reach impact. Once you feel your hip colliding with the shaft at the same moment your clubhead reaches the impact position, it's time to actually hit balls—while still trying to bump the shaft with your hip (fig. 7-15, right).

The ball doesn't lie. If you can hit serviceable shots while causing your hip to clear out and touch the shaft, your lower-body work is excellent. A final tip: if you're having trouble, it may be because you are "losing" your trunk angle (raising up) late in the downswing. If your upper body rises, your hip will not be able to move back and contact the shaft.

3. Slide to the Shaft
The first two drills are designed, at least in part, to incorporate a more emphatic weight shift to the left side on the downswing so

FIG. 7-16. Place the teaching shaft so that it provides a left shift goal (left). On the down-swing, strive to reach the shaft prior to impact, with an emphasis on turning the lower body (middle). Through impact and follow-through, the shaft should remain undisturbed (right).

you arc in a dynamic position at impact. The lack of a full, complete weight shift is by far the most common lower-body problem we encounter. But the weight shift isn't just a matter of moving and turning your hips; it's also a matter of doing it *correctly*. Students sometimes "overcook" an action to the extent they don't perform it properly. The following drill ensures that it is done correctly.

Place the same shaft used in the "Clear-Out Drill" in the ground about 3 inches to the left of the outer portion of your left heel (fig. 7-16, left). Complete your setup, then hit balls using your 5-iron. Your objective is to move your left hip to the shaft as impact approaches so it touches the shaft lightly (fig. 7-16, middle). *The hip should not move beyond the shaft*, however, or you will knock it away from vertical (fig. 7-16, right).

FIG. 7-17. With the ball forward, the Pro can move into the shot (left). When the ball is positioned too far back in the stance, you are forced to strike the shot using your upper body alone (right). Note the lack of lower body movement.

Sometimes, in the effort to move your hips sufficiently to the left, you may slide them forward without turning as you should. When that happens, the lower body gets in the way of the upper body, resulting in a nasty block to the right or a shot struck "fat." Remember, you must both shift and turn to clear your hips, with an assist from your legs, to allow your upper body to move unhindered through impact.

COMMON IMPACT PROBLEMS

Since impact is only a position, all the major problems are position oriented. As with the top of the swing, these problems are a result of what has been done before this position has been reached.

Problem 1. Ball Too Far Back in Stance

Most of the mechanical failures that creep into the swing are visible at impact. Of these, placing the ball too far back in the stance at address is one of the most common and devastating. If the ball is positioned too far to your right at setup, there is no impetus to transfer your weight to the left on the downswing (fig. 7-17). You can hit the ball using your upper body alone (an error countless golfers commit), but your shots will lack power and will suffer in terms of accuracy.

Placing the ball too far back results from not knowing how to perform the transition move and weight shift properly. It is a natural compensation that allows you to at least make contact, albeit poorly. But the consequences are severe. You effectively eliminate all chance for the hips to be vigorously included in the swing. And, of course, if the hips don't get out of the way, the arms can't follow the proper downswing path.

All the impact drills we recommend address this problem effectively. Take stock of your ball position, adjust it as we recommend in the Setup chapter, then perform each of the drills. You'll see improvement right away.

Problem 2. Returning to Your Setup Position

The old concept of "returning to your address position" is outdated and tends to result in a weak, ineffectual impact position. None of the tour players we examined come close to emulating (at impact) the position they occupied at address.

If you were to assume the same position at impact as you did at address, the clubhead would bot-

FIG. 7-18. To generate maximum clubhead speed, the Pro moves the body far in front of the setup position at impact (top). The body position of the student at impact resembles address—static lower body and hands stationed too far behind the ball (bottom). A recipe for weak shots.

Square

Open

Square

Closed

tom out well behind the ball (fig. 7-18). Be sure to use your lower body and upper right side on the downswing. That will ensure that you arrive at impact correctly, with your lower body well forward of where it was at setup. All the impact drills will help produce this result.

Problem 3. Grip Is Too Weak

If you combine a neutral grip with the correct impact position, the clubface will be wide open, forcing all shots to the right. In order to square the clubface, you are forced to rotate your hands desperately as the clubhead nears the ball. This type of clubface manipulation is impossible to time correctly, resulting in shots that may go anywhere (fig. 7-19).

If you are a clubface manipulator, review the "Impact Is Not Setup" section and make sure you use the model grip we described in the Grip chapter. That will guarantee a square clubface at impact.

RELAX AND ENJOY THE VIEW

You're nearing the end of your training for a model swing. Once you've learned to arrive at impact in a dynamic, powerful mode, all you need to do from there is relax. The momentum of the downswing will carry you into a full, free finish. Of course, there are things you can learn from observing your follow-through. That's what the next chapter is all about.

Chapter Eight

Follow-Through

THE MEASURE OF SUCCESS

The ball is long gone, soaring to the target in a majestic parabola. You have experienced the solidity of a sound setup, performed the backswing to perfection, executed a well-timed transition, and arrived at the top with the club set firmly in place. You've torn into the ball with a powerful, coordinated downswing and experienced the euphoric sensation of impact. All there is to do now is admire the perfect shot you just produced. Right?

Well, not quite. Although there's no retrieving a shot once it has left the clubface, the follow-through, nevertheless, is an extremely important part of the full swing. More than any other stage of the swing, it offers unequivocal proof of what your body and club did before the ball was struck. If you sliced, you'll know it by the position of the clubface, your arms, and even your feet as the swing concludes. If you

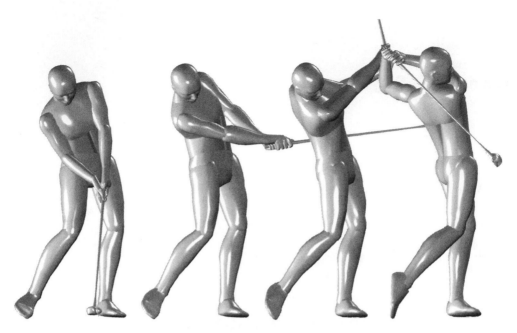

FIG. 8-1. All of the successes and failures of the swing can be seen in the fol-low-through. The Pro follows the ball off the tee with graceful balance.

topped the ball or hit it fat, the cause will reveal itself through a variety of postimpact club and body features. You name the error, the follow-through will reveal it. Whereas impact explains several details about the quality of your downswing, the follow-through explains almost everything (fig. 8-1).

To this point, you may have detected a certain unyielding insistence on our part that the swing be put together in a specific way. If that's the case, so be it. Scientific analysis indicates that the positions and motions that produce a model swing are absolute and shouldn't be compromised. Our view of the follow-through, however, is a bit more relaxed. It is the one stage of the swing where you can display enough idiosyncrasies to make your swing stylish and distinct from those of other players.

The fact that Tiger Woods's follow-through looks nothing like Phil Mickelson's may plant the notion that their swings are nothing alike.

Aesthetically, they are miles apart. Woods's follow-through is full yet somewhat mechanical looking, whereas Mickelson's is softer, more relaxed and natural. But those stylish differences are, for the most part, cosmetic and don't have any real bearing on the swing. If you look closely at their follow-throughs, you'll find that players even as visually different as Woods and Mickelson actually have a lot more in common than you might have initially observed.

It is those common features we'll focus on here. There are a host of follow-through characteristics that are meaningful and have a direct cause/effect relationship with the movements that transpired earlier in the swing. Every good golfer displays these features.

THE SLIDING RIGHT FOOT

On the backswing, the left heel rises ever so slightly to allow a full shift and turn. Late in the downswing, the right heel comes off the ground to allow the right side to power through impact. Although both heels rise at different stages of the swing before impact, it's a tenet of golf that the feet don't slide. That "rule," however, is broken on the follow-through.

Soon after the ball is gone, the left leg remains firmly planted and virtually extended, providing a firm base of support. In contrast, the right foot and leg have been driven toward the target, with the right foot actually sliding forward on its toe (fig. 8-2). The shifting and turning of the hips occurs with so much speed, and their position moves so far to the left, that it carries the right foot along with it.

This is a small but noticeable feature of the game's greatest players. Billy Casper, who won fifty-three Tour tournaments and three major championships, slid his right foot to the left so dramatically that it sometimes collided with his left foot. Of the top contemporary players, Greg Norman

FIG. 8-2. The Pro drives the right side through impact (blue) so dramatically that the right foot is pulled forward during the follow-through (gray).

slides the right foot forward on the follow-through most dramatically. As is the case in all the follow-through actions, the right-foot slide is a result of good swing mechanics. In this case, the strong lower-body shift and turn, coupled with the powerful right-side action leading to impact, produces the foot slide as the swing winds down. The best players don't force the foot forward; their swing automatically does it for them.

A C IS BETTER THAN AVERAGE

From impact to the end of the swing, the upper body continues to "clear" by turning toward the target. Eventually the right side overtakes the left, with your right hand, elbow, and shoulder moving closer to the target than their left-side counterparts. With the hips shifted well toward the target, and your head near its initial position, the end result of these actions is that your body takes on a curved appearance resembling the letter *C* in reverse (fig. 8-3). This is the "look" you want.

Although your head remains even with your ball position while the hips have moved ahead of that point, the aggressiveness of the movement has shifted your weight almost entirely onto your left side. There's no hanging back on your right side here.

FIG. 8-3. The lower body is so active that it forms a reverse C during the follow-through. It is important to note that the Pro achieves this position by moving the lower body forward, not by moving the upper body backward.

EXPLODING TWO MYTHS

Deep into the follow-through, the right side continues to move ahead of the left. At that point, two fascinating characteristics become apparent, shattering forever two myths regarding the swing.

First, the left elbow is still visible above the right (fig. 8-4). That explodes the old belief that the left elbow should be tucked close to the side of the body at impact and into the follow-through. It was widely thought that "letting the left arm fold" was an efficient means of squaring the clubface at impact. A closer study of top players reveals that "tucking" the left elbow into your side isn't necessary. You should allow the momentum of your arms to carry them away from your upper body. The clubface squares itself through sound swing mechanics and a correct grip.

Second, the head has swiveled forward, following the turning action of the upper body (fig. 8-5). So much for the old adage, "Keep your head down after the ball is gone." By freeing up your head, and letting it turn of its own accord on the follow-through, you allow the upper body to complete its turn into a full, unrestricted finish. If you consciously attempt to keep your head down, with your eyes glued to the ground after impact, you impose a limit on your upper-body freedom.

The problem with those golfers who mistakenly attempt to freeze their head at impact is that it affects the entire swing, not just the fol-

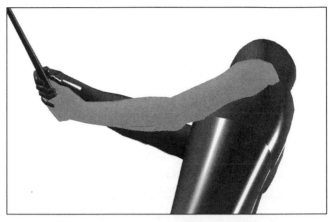

FIG. 8-4. The Pro allows the momentum of the follow-through to naturally extend the left arm (blue).

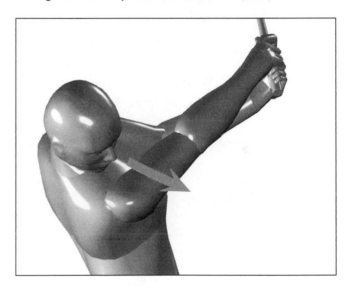

FIG. 8-5. The Pro produces a free-turning follow-through by following the ball off the tee.

low-through. If you decide, in advance, that your eyes must continue to watch the ground after the ball is gone, you will change your entire swing in order to make it happen. Experience has shown that to accomplish this goal, a weak, arm-dominated swing is required.

SQUARE THE CLUBFACE NATURALLY

Looking down the target line, you can see how the left side continues to "clear out" to allow the right side to swing through to the finish (fig. 8-6). Note also that, even this late in the swing, the head still hasn't risen from the position it occupied throughout the swing. Those are key points. The most interesting aspect of the follow-through from this angle, however, is the myth-busting relationship among the hands, wrists, and forearms.

Note that the two hands and wrists are not "crossed over," with the right hand twisted atop the left. This is proof that you do not need (or want) to consciously rotate your hands and arms through impact as a means of squaring the clubface. That's what a crossed-over look indicates—too much hand and forearm rotation—and it's a true swing killer. Trying to rotate the clubface to a square position through a last-second "snap" of the hands is a recipe for wildness and inconsistency. Who can consistently time and control the rotation of an object that is moving upward of 100 miles per hour? The fact that the best players don't try it may give you some idea of the difficulty of this maneuver.

FIG. 8-6. The Pro knows better than to try to manipulate the clubface angle during the swing by crossing the forearms. A model swing allows him to avoid this unnatural compensation.

One of the most interesting discoveries in our study was how little the better players manipulated the clubface. It is not surprising, in retrospect, because a minuscule alteration in face angle can make a major difference in the shot result. The most successful players quickly found a way to swing so that they had to make virtually no alteration in clubface angle. As mentioned in previous chapters, this is the main reason for the strong grip and slightly closed clubface throughout the swing. The follow-through again demonstrates this fact, since the clubface shows no sign of manipulation even at the end of the swing.

Years of instruction have taught us that it

is the high-handicap players who alter the clubface angle. As impact approaches, they find themselves in a poor position, giving them a face-angle adjustment as the only last-second method to save the shot. Sometimes it works, sometimes it doesn't. It doesn't take many failures to ruin a round of golf.

Through intelligent, correct use of your legs, torso, hands, and arms during the swing, the clubface will arrive at the ball in a square position of its own accord, without undue manipulation on your part.

A BALANCED FINISH

Although your body positions have changed dramatically by the time the swing is completed, they consistently reflect the soundness of the motions that occurred earlier. Every part of the body has played a specific, vital role in the swing, and it shows. No single part of the anatomy has out-performed or overshadowed the others. The best follow-throughs have a dreamlike quality to them, an aesthetic blend of speed, grace, and technical proficiency.

From the face-on view, you can see how the lower body has rotated to its farthest comfortable extreme, while the upper body has rotated almost 90 degrees left of the target (fig. 8-7, left). You can also see how the upper body, fueled by the powerful right-side movement that began early in the downswing, has rotated so far that the right shoulder is much closer to the target than the left. The head, respond-

FIG. 8-7. As the follow-through concludes, the face-on view shows how the Pro has finally driven the right side past the left (left). The down-the-line view demonstrates that the extreme lower body rotation now has the hips facing the target, while the shoulders have finally caught and rotated past the hips (right).

ing to the movement of the upper body, has released and turned to a position where you can observe the ball.

Finally, the momentum of the arms has carried them to a point that is now farthest from the target, with the club wrapped well around the back of the body. Just a moment earlier they were the part of the body *closest* to the target, a testament to how fast they were moving. Viewed from down-the-target line, the same powerful rotation is apparent, with the two knees and the hips facing the target (fig. 8-7, right).

The word to describe the perfect follow-through is "balance," because it applies both literally and figuratively. Despite the furious activity that brought the swing to its conclusion, your weight should be so well distributed that it would require a healthy push to knock you off your feet.

LET IT HAPPEN

As was the case late in the downswing, if the preparation was sound, the follow-through should just happen. All the critical results are due to just getting the body out of the way of the clubhead and not trying to artificially affect the swing.

THE FOLLOW-THROUGH DRILLS

In a sense, the drills we've designed are not follow-through drills at all. Because the follow-through is only the by-product of sound preimpact club and body motions, the drills we've created are designed to improve your entire swing. Still, they provide the best, most accurate checks to ensure that you've delivered the club and your body to a full, correct finish.

1. Eyes on the Ball
As we discussed earlier, the most overused piece of advice in golf is the phrase "Keep your head still and your eyes on the ball." Not

only is it overused, it is dead wrong. Keeping your eyes riveted on the spot the ball occupied before you struck it severely stifles a free release of your upper body on the follow-through. And it doesn't do much for your downswing, either.

When you practice, go ahead and keep your eyes on the ball, *especially after it leaves the clubface* (fig. 8-8). Try not to lose eye contact with the ball. That's an impossible task, of course—even the best players fall behind—but the idea is to allow your head to swivel forward along with your shoulders. Two of the better young players in golf today, David Duval and Annika Sorenstam, actually give the impression they are lifting their heads too soon on the follow-through. In fact, they are merely allowing their heads to rise so they can track the flight of the ball with their eyes. And they both have extremely free movement of their upper bodies, allowing them full, unrestricted finishes.

2. Toe Points Up

Another problem noted earlier is the tendency to square the clubface by snapping, or rolling, the hands and wrists through impact. This last-second attempt to rotate the clubface closed is as fatal as it is desperate, because not one player in a million can perform such a delicate maneuver with any consistency. The only way to square the clubface consistently and accurately is through the correct grip and proper blend of body, arm, and hand action during the swing.

How well are you releasing the club? Here's a good check: with a short iron, hit shots at ³/₄ speed, terminating the swing soon after impact when the shaft of the club is parallel with the ground (fig. 8-9). Hold your finish and inspect the position of the clubhead. The toe of the club should be pointing at the sky. That's proof you've rotated the club to square by using your body, arms, and hands *together*, not just your forearms and hands alone. If the clubhead is "flipped over," with the face of the club pointing at the ground, you've rotated your hands excessively.

Once you have gained control of your clubface, the next focus

Square

FIG. 8-8. By allowing your head to swivel after impact, your upper body can turn into a full, unrestrained finish.

FIG. 8-9. If you can make the toe of the club point to the sky midway into the follow-through, you've mastered a correct release through impact.

must be on ball flight. If you find your shots going to the right, then you haven't properly prepared your swing prior to impact. In this case, check that your grip is sufficiently strong and that you're keeping the face slightly closed during the entire swing.

If your shots are going left and fading back to the target, it's a sure sign that you're not using your lower body correctly. This results in an arm-dominated swing that invariably produces the dreaded over-the-top move and the outside-to-inside swing path. In this case, return to the basics and work on developing a total body swing.

FIG. 8-10. In the Cover the Shaft drill, your goal is to conceal the club placed on the ground outside your left foot (left). The club should respond to the movement of your body by tracking to the inside on the follow-through (right).

3. Cover the Shaft

A common tendency, especially among players who want more accuracy, is to "guide" the clubhead through impact so it extends down the target line as far as possible. At the same time, they try to hold the clubface in a square position at impact and beyond, "blocking" the ball forcefully to the target. This method, while instinctive, fights the natural movement of your body and isn't all that accurate to begin with. The following check will improve your method of naturally releasing the club through impact and beyond.

Place a club on the ground, just outside the ball and aligned directly at the target (fig. 8-10, left). Now put down a second club, this one running from the outside of your left little toe on a line parallel to the first club. Assuming your setup position, turn slowly into your follow-through and, at the point when the club you are holding is parallel to the ground, make it "cover" the club on the ground that is aligned with your toes (fig. 8-10, right). Return to your setup position and repeat three times, each time concealing the shaft on the ground with the club in your hands. Commit the sensation to memory. Now hit some shots at partial speed, stopping your finish to inspect if you are "covering" the shaft on the ground.

To fulfill the requirements of the drill, you should allow the club to move inside the target line after impact, following your body as it also turns to the left. This is the correct, natural way to swing the club through impact into the follow-through. Never try to guide the ball by swinging the clubhead straight down the target line. Let the club follow your body, and the accuracy business will eventually take care of itself.

If you find that your club is coming out closer to the shaft aligned with the ball, you can bet you're not sufficiently turning your lower body into the shot. Note that the key to success in this movement lies with the lower body, not the arms. Use the lower body correctly and you will give the arms the ability to perform the correct movement.

4. Knees Together

To arrive at impact in a sound, powerful position, the upper and lower body must work in unison with each other. How well they perform relative to each other is apparent on the follow-through. For example, if your upper body outraces your lower body, it will be apparent in the twisted, off-balance follow-through "look" that ensues after the ball is gone.

One of the simplest ways to check the cooperative movement of the upper and lower body is to examine the position of your knees on the follow-through. Make a normal full swing and, at the finish of your follow-through, freeze the position of your lower body. Look down. Your knees should be close together, with both kneecaps the same distance from the target (fig. 8-11). If your right knee hasn't drawn even with the left knee, it probably means you've failed to properly use the lower body, forcing the upper body and arms to dominate the swing. It indicates a poor transition move and a poor sequence of movement on the downswing.

Perform this inspection often. The key to obtaining the correct knee relationship is to shift and rotate your hips aggressively on the downswing so you can fire "down and through" with your right side.

5. Left Leg Only

One of the most common errors in golf is the dreaded "reverse pivot," whereby your weight stays left on the backswing, then moves right on the downswing—exactly the opposite move of the better golfer. You don't have to commit this error to an extreme for it to affect your swing; even keeping a relatively small percentage of your weight on the right side at the end of the swing can upset the correct motion. The following inspection drill will immediately tell you how well you are shifting your weight during the transition and downswing.

Hit a ball in routine fashion and, at the completion of your follow-through, hold your position. Now simply lift your right foot off the ground (fig. 8-12). Can you balance on your left leg alone? If you transferred your weight fully and correctly, it should be no problem. If you can't do it, here's a tip: finish so only the toe of your right foot is touching the ground, your hips and knees are facing the target, and your left leg is straight.

COMMON FOLLOW-THROUGH PROBLEMS

Most of the typical follow-through problems are simply a result of errors made earlier in the swing. Since these are results, not causes, they will not be addressed here. There are three problems, however, that are

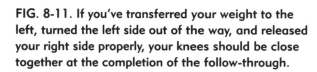

FIG. 8-11. If you've transferred your weight to the left, turned the left side out of the way, and released your right side properly, your knees should be close together at the completion of the follow-through.

FIG. 8-12. Another sign of a full shifting of weight to the left is your ability to hoist your right foot off the ground—and hold it there—at the conclusion of the follow-through.

a direct result of trying to do something incorrectly during the final stages of the swing.

Problem 1. Why Chickens Don't Fly

If you fail to move your lower body and right side into the shot, a slew of unwanted results occur. The most damaging is the production of a steep, outside-to-inside arm and clubhead path, which places you in a no-win situation. If you continue to swing along the poor path and allow your shoulders and arms to follow through correctly, all your shots will go to the left. Your only choice is to keep the left arm above the right, which opens the clubface and slices the ball back toward the target (fig. 8-13, left).

FIG. 8-13. A photo of the student just after impact (left) shows he has curtailed the normal release of the arms and clubface to avoid pulling the ball to the left. The end result, the chicken wing finish (right), is a familiar sight to every golfer.

This high left arm attempt to save the shot results in what is typically called a "chicken wing" follow-through (fig. 8-13, right), which is not caused by the arms but by the lack of lower body and right-side movement. If you see this in your swing, make the "Cover the Shaft," "Knees Together," and "Left Leg Only" drills a part of your practice routine.

Problem 2. Keep Your Head Down
When all else fails, golfers resort to blaming the inability to "keep the head down" as the cause of all that is wrong with a golf swing. Although this may have some merit during the backswing, this thought has no usefulness in the follow-through (fig. 8-14).

FIG. 8-14. The Pro allows a full release by following the ball off the tee (left). The student (right) has followed the tradition of keeping his head down, severely restricting the body rotation both before and after impact.

If you have overextended this concept into your follow-through, use the "Eyes on the Ball" drill to liberate your body after impact.

Problem 3. Slam the Face Shut

For whatever reason, if your clubface is open during the downswing, you are forced to slam the face closed at the last moment to save the shot (fig. 8-15). Experience has shown that this correction begins about $\frac{1}{30}$ of a second before impact and can involve changing the face angle up to 90 degrees.

The fact that the best athletes in the world go to great lengths to avoid changing the face angle at all should indicate the folly of trying to live with this problem. This is one of the

FIG. 8-15. The Proper grip allows the Pro to simply swing through impact without altering the club-face (left). An open clubface, due to a weak grip (or some other cause), forces you to rotate the club furiously at the last second in order to hit the ball straight. This results in a closed clubface during the follow-through (right). The fact that the clubface could be open, square, or closed at impact means that the ball may go anywhere.

few swing errors that don't produce predictable results. If you close the face too much, the shot will go left. If you fail to close it enough, the shot goes right. You may be able to live with a problem like a predictable slice or a hook, but this one needs to be avoided at all costs. Use the "Toe Points Up" drill to eliminate this disastrous move in your swing.

SUMMARY: RIGHT IS MIGHT

The great majority of poor follow-through positions are rooted in the same cause: failure to utilize your lower body and right side correctly and forcefully on the downswing. The pervasive nature of these problems may stem from the old teaching philosophy that the left side "controls" the downswing and the right shoulder, arm, and hand are "bad guys" that need reining in. In fact, the entire right side of your body, when used correctly, is not only a tremendous power producer but a source of accuracy as well.

No less a player than Ben Hogan stated, "As far as applying power goes, I wish I had three right hands." Hogan and every other good player has learned to impart as much energy as possible with the right side, using the left side for guidance and support. The key is to involve the *entire right side,* for if you rely on your hands and arms alone to square the clubface and supply power, you'll be doomed to a lifetime of inconsistency.

THE LAST PIECES OF THE PUZZLE

With every mechanical detail of a perfect swing now in place, only two ingredients remain to be added: timing and tempo. It is these two factors that "oil" the machine you've created, that inject smoothness, coordination, and consistency into every swing. Incorporate the information from the next chapter and your education on the full swing will be complete.

Chapter Nine

Timing and Tempo

BLENDING THE PACKAGE TOGETHER

Ben Hogan was once queried by an equipment manufacturer about why he refused to play the company's ball, which was used by many other professionals. Hogan told them the ball was inferior. The company, confident it could win Hogan over, flew him to their plant and allowed him to observe while they ran the ball through a variety of tests, the most impressive of which involved hitting the ball with a robotlike hitting machine.

The machine, which at the time was state of the art, did not "swing" the club. It was fixed in what amounts to a top-of-swing position, a club clamped into place so a perfect strike was guaranteed. A switch was thrown and the machine channeled the club through the ball. Every shot was exactly the same.

Hogan, nonplussed, watched the machine hit several balls. The

FIG. 9-1. Putting the whole swing together so it flows is an exercise in producing the proper timing and tempo.

company executives, flushed with success, beamed as they told Hogan, "Ben, you can't get more advanced than that."

Replied Hogan, "If that's the case, then I recommend you enter the driving machine in the U.S. Open."

The point was well made. Human beings are not robots, and perfect swing mechanics aren't everything. Sophisticated as the driving contraption may have been, it was made of metal, not flesh and blood. It had far fewer moving parts than the human body. The machine didn't have to worry about ball position, the many nuances of the correct grip, getting the backswing under way, or making a great transition move.

Most important, the machine didn't have to worry about timing and tempo, which may be the two most elusive parts of the swing. After you've acquired a thorough understanding of the correct positions and movements, you need a way to blend them together into one continuous, unified action that is devoid of choppiness, strain, or exertion. That's what timing and tempo do. They are the glue that binds the mechanical aspects of the swing together, while at the same time allowing them full expression (fig. 9-1).

Though apparent to the naked eye, timing and tempo are extremely difficult for the average golfer to master. In some ways, they are regarded the same as someone with musical talent—you either have it or you don't. That is not the case, however. Many people with no natural athleticism have succeeded in building swings that have a smooth, dreamlike quality to them while also being sound mechanically.

In golf instruction parlance, timing and tempo are sometimes used synonymously. In fact, their meanings are quite different. *Timing* is the order in which the body parts move to cause the club to arrive at the ball in perfect position (fig. 9-2). It describes the sequence of movements that allows the body parts to work in harmony with one another, to deploy the club in the most dynamic, efficient manner possible. Good timing allows your body to perform with almost hydraulic strength and economy, so the energy you expend is not wasted, but multiplied.

Tempo, on the other hand, merely describes the overall pace of the swing (fig. 9-3). It is just as important, for it has the capability of enhancing your timing or ruining it. If your swing is too fast (a rarity, in our opinion), the body parts have difficulty working in concert with another. Parts of your anatomy are brought into play before they should be, or else join in too late. If your swing is too slow and deliberate (as are most swings), the motion loses much-needed momentum. Important swing positions are forced into place rather than flowing together. The swing becomes labored, awkward, and static.

A great many golfers work extremely hard at

FIG. 9-2. Timing is the order in which movements occur. Building the proper sequence throughout the swing allows the entire movement to flow together in a seemingly effortless manner.

FIG. 9-3. Tempo is the speed at which the swing occurs. Controlling the tempo allows the Pro the time to properly prepare for impact, deliver an explosive blow to the ball, then dissipate the momentum of the swing during the follow-through.

mastering great mechanics, while paying little attention to timing and tempo. It's as if they believe they'll succeed through sheer effort, persistence, and attention to every technical detail. In truth, if you add a bit of smoothness and artistry to your swing by improving your timing and tempo, your mechanics will improve as a result.

TIMING: FOUR BASIC MOVES

The total number of movements involved in the golf swing is awesome. There are far too many to count, let alone describe for inclusion into the swing. Performing the golf swing is much like driving a car—you want to keep your eyes riveted on a spot well ahead of you and allow your subconscious to relay the tiny corrective movements of the

FIG. 9-4. The initial shift is dominated by a lateral move to the right during the first half of the backswing.

FIG. 9-5. The Pro makes the first turn around the right leg during the second half of the backswing.

steering wheel to your hands. If you thought about each individual movement, you'd crash.

For our purposes, know that there are four major motions that shape and control the swing: it begins with a *shift,* which is followed by a *turn,* which is followed by a second *shift,* and which concludes with another *turn.* If you can improve your performance of those motions individually, and refine the manner in which one flows into the next, your timing can't help but improve.

The Initial Shift

As we described in the Backswing chapter, the first body shift occurs as you move from the setup position to the point where the clubshaft is parallel to the ground (fig. 9-4). This is primarily a lateral movement and is performed by shifting our entire body to the right. Your hands

FIG. 9-6. The second shift emphasizes the weight shift back to the left side during transition and the beginning of the downswing.

FIG. 9-7. The Pro finishes a model swing by rotating around the left side.

at this point are doing nothing except holding on to the club. The lateral body shift is small, only about 2 inches, but it is enough to transfer nearly all your weight onto your right side and prepare your body to accept the next movement.

The First Turn

Now it is time to blend some rotary motion into the swing. At the moment the clubshaft is parallel to the ground, you want to turn your body fully around your right leg, which serves as the axis (fig. 9-5). Virtually all of the turn should take place by the time the clubshaft reaches a vertical position.

The first turn is critical in regard to timing. You must not allow your body to shift too far laterally to the right, or it becomes impossible to shift your weight back to the left in a coordinated fashion.

The Second Shift

It is now time for the transition move, which is dominated by a lateral shifting of the hips back to the left (fig. 9-6). This is probably the most critical timing movement of all, since it involves a change of direction. The transition move takes lots of practice to integrate smoothly into your swing.

The Second Turn

Once the transition move has carried you into the downswing, you should have only one thought: to turn around the left side as fast as you can and to get out of the way and allow the arms and club to follow the proper path to the ball (fig. 9-7). If you performed the transition move correctly, you don't need to worry about your swing getting out of sync. The stage is set, and you want to concentrate on turning your right side down and through impact.

It's a Feeling

It would be nice if the golf swing was as simple as shift-turn-shift-turn. In fact, when the swing is being dominated by a shift, turning is also happening. During the initial shift, the arms are moved by a slight hip and shoulder turn. Likewise, when turning is the dominant move, some shifting is occurring. During the transition, hip turn is used to twist the powerful trunk muscles to prepare them for their powerful contribution in the downswing.

What you want to feel in your swing is the rhythmic sensation of shift-turn-shift-turn (fig. 9-8). If done properly, all the other supporting movements will fall into place.

TEMPO: THE SLOWEST 2 SECONDS IN HISTORY

One of the most startling revelations of our research was how quickly the entire swing takes place. There is a long-standing notion that the swing

FIG. 9-8. The entire swing timing is combined with an integration of the shift (left), turn (middle left), shift (middle right), turn (right). If done in the proper sequence, the movements become seamless.

should be long, languid, and deliberate. Yet the more than one hundred pros we examined proved that is not the case. It took, on average, only 1 second to transport the club from address to impact. The follow-through took another second, for a total elapsed time of only *2 seconds* (fig. 9-9).

How can top professionals perform the swing in such a short period of time, yet give the appearance of swinging so slowly and smoothly? The answer is that they perform all the movements correctly. The technical excellence of their positions, combined with the fine manner in which they flow together, gives the illusion of slowness. It's only when a swing gets out of kilter that it looks unduly fast.

There is no single tempo that is good for all players. Everyone is slightly different. The tempo you adopt probably will reflect your personality, and that's fine. A high-strung, fidgety person probably will

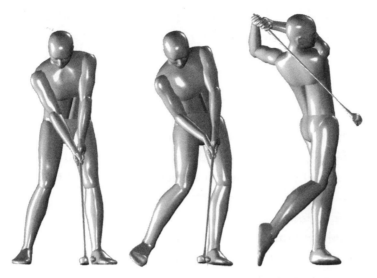

FIG. 9-9. The Pro moves from setup (left) to impact (middle) in only 1 second, then finishes the follow-through in another second (right). Although this 2 second interval is very fast, the error-free swing of the Pro makes the movement appear effortless.

swing faster than someone who is naturally more relaxed. It's wise not to fight your natural tempo tendency. If Lanny Wadkins, whose swing is very fast, tried to swing like Ernie Els, who is quite slow, it would wreck his game.

The key is in qualifying "fast" and "slow." Out of all the pros analyzed, the slowest took only about ½ second longer to reach impact than the fastest. The problem most developing golfers have is not in finding their tempo, for that's genetically built into each player. The problem is allowing their natural tempo to emerge. We have seen numerous students try to control the club so much that their swing moves in slow motion. It's not uncommon for this type of golfer to take more time to move through the first *third* of his backswing then it takes a good player to complete the entire swing.

Your goal should be to build a golf swing that will allow you to reach your own, best tempo.

TIMING AND TEMPO DRILLS

Since both timing and tempo are "whole-swing" feelings, the drills to get these feelings across must be the same. The goal is to have the swing parts flow together, in the proper sequence and at the correct pace.

1. Pick a Part

Your ability to time the swing depends a great deal on how well you perform the four basic swing movements (the two shifts and the two turns). Done correctly, it becomes much easier to blend them together into one uninterrupted, flowing movement. The purpose of this drill—actually, you can devote an entire practice session to it—is to isolate each of the four basic motions, performing them one at a time and monitoring the results.

Start by isolating the initial body shift (fig. 9-10). Hit ten balls, thinking of nothing except the proper execution of that move. For emphasis, say "shift" out loud the moment you begin the swing.

Progress through each of the four basic movements, hitting ten balls for each one. If you need some external feedback, you can use the teaching shaft to bump up against or turn around. Perform this exercise often, paying special attention to the area that needs the most work. Your timing will improve very rapidly.

2. See It, Do It

How often have you had the following experience? You have attended a golf tournament and watched the tour players with their rhythmic, seemingly effortless but powerful swings. When you return home and finally have the opportunity to get to the golf course, you find the rhythm and tempo of the professionals has

FIG. 9-10. Work through the swing one section at a time, beginning with the initial shift. Think "shift," as you move from setup (left) into the backswing (right). Complete the swing without further thought.

somehow seeped into your swing. You play some of the best golf of your life in the next two days. You may not have paid attention to the specific mechanics used by the players you observed, yet your swing mysteriously has improved dramatically.

This phenomenon is what educational psychologists call "modeling," or observational learning, one of the most effective modes of processing information, *if* you have the appropriate model to observe on a consistent basis. Unfortunately, most of us can't follow the tour from tournament to tournament. We need a way to get our "booster shots" of appropriate swing models.

The solution is to perform what sports psychologists call "visuo-motor rehearsal." It begins by you selecting as your model a fine, low-handicap player from your club (if you belong to one), or

FIG. 9-11. Pick a tour player and just watch the tempo of the swing.

FIG. 9-12. Watch the fluid movements from several viewpoints.

videotaping the swing of your favorite professional (fig. 9-11; Ernie Els is a fine example). Watch it closely, at least five times. Then close your eyes and rehearse in your own mind the swing you have watched your player perform. Forget his swing mechanics. Instead, try to get a sense or "feel" of the swing as a whole, concentrating on the player's smoothness, timing, and tempo.

Imagine yourself as that player. Feel yourself making the same swing, emulating the great pace and rhythm. If you can videotape your favorite player from several angles, so much the better (fig. 9-12). Let your subconscious mind soak up the wonderful swing in its entirety. As you perform these make-believe swings, rehearse how your body will feel when you actually make the swing yourself.

You can combine this visuo-motor rehearsal with actually swinging a real golf club. Go through the same mental learning process, then set up and take five swings, thinking only of repeating the same tempo you just saw in your mind's eye.

Whether you swing or not, you will experience significant learning gains. The important variable is repetition. Conduct the exercise often, whether sitting at your desk at work or relaxing at home.

3. Tempo Master

If you want to get an idea about the tempo of your swing, this drill is for you. Set the teaching metronome described in the Teaching Introduction at a 2-second interval. On the practice tee, using your 9-iron, set up in your normal manner. Close your eyes and listen to the 2-second beat. Feel yourself starting the swing on the first beat, then finishing on the second. If the tempo is too slow or too fast, try adjusting it to fit your natural feeling. Do not, however, set the tempo faster than 1.5 seconds or slower than 2.5 seconds.

Once you find a comfortable tempo, open your eyes and try swinging the club, without a ball. Start the swing on one beat and finish on the next. It will take some time to get the tempo down, but you will eventually feel the rhythm of the swing.

Once you feel comfortable with the tempo, hit some balls (fig. 9-13). Begin with the metronome on, then turn it off. After several practice sessions, your tempo should become a natural part of your swing.

If you feel confident with your 9-iron, move to the longer clubs. There is no need to change anything; the tempo for all your clubs is the same.

After each session, write down the time that you discovered best fit your swing. Always begin

FIG. 9-13. With the metronome set on your chosen tempo, begin your swing on one beat, then try to finish on the second.

the drill using the 2-second interval, then change it to fit how you feel that day. If you continue to finish with the same result, you have found your tempo. Our experience indicates that as your swing improves, your tempo will increase. It's not that your natural tempo changes; it's that your improved swing allows you to finally play with your inherited rhythm.

COMMON TIMING AND TEMPO PROBLEMS

Since timing and tempo are related to the whole swing, there are thousands of ways to disrupt how you put the components together (timing) and how fast you execute each one (tempo). Experience has

FIG. 9-14. The Pro has completed the initial shift, the initial turn, and has begun the second shift with the proper timing (left). The student started the initial shift too late, disrupting the timing of the swing and making it impossible to recover from this poor position (right).

shown, however, that there are certain errors commonly made that can disrupt the natural flow of the swing.

Problem 1. Timing Breaks

Any time the shift-turn-shift-turn sequence is broken, disaster results. The biggest problem develops, however, when breaks occur early in the swing (fig. 9-14). If you don't make the initial shift off the ball, you will be forced to shift later in the backswing. If you shift this late in the swing, it delays your emphasis on the first turn, which eliminates any hope for a transition and disrupts the final shift and turn. If this sounds like a swing out of control, it is. This is a common high-handicap problem.

The second most common timing error is the elimination of the second shift. If the transition is not performed, the most powerful portion of the swing is missing. It's not as disrupting as the first example, but it results in a decided loss of both distance and consistency. This is typically a middle handicapper's problem.

Both of these problems can be addressed by reviewing the proper moves to the top of the swing (chapters 1–5), then putting them all together with the "Pick a Part" drill.

Problem 2. Tempo Breaks

The great majority of developing golfers swing too slowly because most are trying to fix their swing problems by manipulating the club. As your swing improves, however, you will need to begin to trust your swing and let the club move freely. The goal of every golfer should be to move the body so that the club can perform as it was designed. If words don't get this across, simply observe players known for their tempo, like Payne Stewart or Al Geiberger (fig. 9-15).

Use the "See It, Do It" process to improve your feeling of swing tempo and the "Tempo Master" drill to begin to discover your own rhythm. And continue to improve so that you can allow the swing to just happen.

THE BEGINNING, NOT THE END

The end of our presentation on the golf swing may imply that you have reached the end of your journey. In fact, you have just begun. As pointed out in the Teaching Introduction, it takes time and effort to build a better golf swing. But since golf is a lifetime undertaking, you have the time. And now you also have the knowledge. The next step is making the best use of both of these assets. The final chapter addresses your golfing future.

FIG. 9-15. Payne Stewart possesses a natural ability to swing the club with wonderful tempo and rhythm. Repeated observation of these types of swings can give you the feeling of the proper tempo.

Chapter Ten

Swing Like a Pro

DEVELOPING THE SWING OF YOUR DREAMS

We have been studying the golf swing for twenty years, and we continue to discover new insights from both our research and teaching. We hope that you have found this book to be a similar experience; every time you read it you discover something new and exciting. Besides actually playing the game, there is no better feeling than to step on the pratice tee with a new swing thought or drill that you know will improve your swing. And this is but one part of the total golf experience.

Golf is such a diverse game. Proud as we are of our efforts to discover and disseminate the true fundamentals of the full swing, we are very much aware that there is more to the game than hitting the ball far and straight. No matter how well you learn to strike the ball, you will undoubtedly be called upon to utilize many skills not covered in this book. The finer points of the short game, handling difficult lies, deal-

231

ing with the wind, and hitting draws and fades at will have not been covered here. Playing in bad weather, controlling your emotions, developing sound course management, knowing the rules, becoming a tough competitor—those are topics we may cover in the future, and certainly are skills the finished golfer must master if he is to reach his maximum potential.

It is important to remember that golf is, above all, a game. Swing mechanics are extremely important, as the motion required to consistently strike the ball well is tremendously complex and requires a thorough understanding of cause and effect. Yet, as Lee Trevino, one of the greatest players in history, once pointed out, the ability to score well is a matter of advancing the ball from point A (the tee) to point B (the hole) as expeditiously as you can. The game is an art as well as a science, and this fact will become increasingly evident as your swing mechanics improve.

Our objective has been to get your full swing in order, to improve your ball-striking ability to the point where your long-term goals become more attainable. To that end, we would like to add a few final hints to get the most out of what you have read in the preceding chapters.

As you strive to perfect your full swing, you'll find it helpful and stimulating to employ a bit of fun and creativity. Learning is faster and easier when you enjoy what you're doing, so don't hesitate to inject a bit of variety in your practice sessions. Stay faithful to our directives by all means, but intersperse your hard work with a bit of pure fun. On the practice range, try hitting shots with less than full force. See if you can curve the ball in either direction, or high and low, at will. Hit shots from poor lies. Mentally devise makeshift "holes" on the practice range and play them, using the necessary clubs while concentrating on performing the model swing (fig. 10-1).

Play as much as you practice. It is impossible to re-create on the range all the unusual shots you encounter on the course. When you tackle the course and engage in a $5 nassau with your pals, fight any inclination to return to your previous method. Only through dedication and commitment will you groove the fail-safe methods described in this book.

FIG. 10-1. Practice is the key to improvement, but it must be both directed and enjoyable.

GOOD INFORMATION, A PLAN, AND COMMITMENT

So many golfers fail to reach their potential because they either give up too early or don't make the commitment necessary to exact results from the learning program. The desire to obtain fast fixes and honest results without physical effort or intellectual application is what keeps equipment manufacturers and teaching pros in business. The beguiling promises of buying a better game are alluring, certainly more so than long hours, days, and months sweating on the practice tee.

But there is no quick fix, magic move, big-name instructor, or any other source capable of transforming your game overnight. Obviously, you sense this already. You've dedicated yourself to absorbing more than 50,000 well-chosen words. Still, we can't emphasize enough the importance of sticking with our observations, analyses, and hands-on instruction. Results take time, but we can't express the pride and self-satisfaction you'll experience when the fundamentals of the model swing become part and parcel of your game, and noticeable improvement kicks in. We may have provided the information, but it is you who earned the reward. It's a great feeling.

OLD HABITS DIE HARD

Before you can go forward, you must evaluate the state of your golf game and determine your goals for the future. An honest assessment of these factors will help you shape your path to improvement. The necessary time commitments become more apparent. Swing objectives are planned more realistically and real progress becomes easier to track. Most important of all, you gain the ability to identify and overcome bad swing habits.

Every golfer is prone to recurring bad swing habits, just as we experience bad habits in everyday life. They are persistent, crop up without provocation, and are resorted to in moments of sheer hopelessness. Whether your weakness is a craving for chocolates or a tendency to start the downswing by incorrectly moving your shoulders and left arm, it is important to recognize your bad habits. Doing so is the first step to breaking the habit once and for all and replacing it with new movements that are healthy and productive. In order to break these old habits and learn new ones, you must first have a thorough understanding of the swing flaws you want to eliminate.

Second, you must formulate an effective plan for improvement. Broad intentions are good, but until you identify your basic swing problems and outline a program to eliminate them, your game will never progress. We suggest that you start with your grip and setup. Use chapters 1 and 2 to evaluate your weaknesses, as well as the drills to focus on to improve. You will derive great satisfaction as you cross off your initial list of swing flaws.

Once you have the grip and setup mastered, move on to the swing. Work through each part of the swing, identifying then solving your

FIG. 10-2. Regardless of the quality of the player, everyone has swing errors that are difficult to overcome.

own problems. You will find that some portions of the swing are easy, while some will seem to defy all attempts at improvement. When you have taken your swing to follow-through, and integrated timing and tempo, you will be left with a list of several of these persistent errors. Don't despair—even the best players in the world have a list of problems that plague their swing (fig. 10-2).

At this point, you will have solved all of the easy problems, and you will see a jump in the quality of your game. You can now look forward to taking the rest of your golfing life to make improvements in your limited list of persistent swing problems.

Finally, you must have a fierce desire to follow through and accomplish your goals. Understanding and a detailed plan is essential, but if it is not executed the effort is wasted. We can help you better understand both your swing and the improvement process, but only you can make it happen.

We have learned from experience that not all people learn at the same rate. Some people simply process information faster than others do. However long it takes to assimilate the instructional points, you must respect the time it takes and remain patient. Never give up on your effort to improve your game.

CONTINUING EDUCATION

An important question is, what do you do with the information we have presented in the preceding pages? During closing ceremonies at our schools, Phil Rodgers always explains to his students that golf is a difficult game and that you never stop learning. He goes on to talk about how golf instruction is a never-ending education and how everyone in the class is at a different grade level. The learning program dispensed in this book is no different. In order for you to go from one level to the next, you must follow the lesson plan that we have laid out for your improvement.

Consider that the model swing is comprised of ten teaching positions, with the model being perfect in all positions. Assigning a score of 10 points for each position, the model totals 100 points for the entire swing. Each student we teach begins with a certain point total: some score 40 points out of 100, while others achieve 70 or 80 points. Regardless of the grade they display at the outset, the goal is to increase the students' point total every time they come to one of our programs. It is unrealistic to expect a score of 100 points, but if you go from 50 points to 60 over several days, you obviously have made significant improvement. The goal is steady, lasting improvement that holds up and improves further over time. Remember, there is no quick fix or magic move that will get you there overnight. Also remember that you may experience some slight setbacks before you can make noticeable improvements.

SETBACKS: UNDERSTANDING
THE LEARNING CURVE

Anytime you try to process new information or learn a new skill (particularly involving motor skill), it is inevitable that you will experience a slight regression, or setback, during your journey to long-term improvement. We all have built-in compensation factors that enable us to get the ball airborne toward the desired target. For example, someone with an over-the-top, slice-producing swing will instinctively compensate by adopting a stronger grip and aiming to the left of the target. Conversely, someone with a flat, hook-producing swing will adopt a weaker grip, place the ball back in the stance, and aim to the right of the target. In order to accomplish long-term improvement in your game, these compensations must be minimized.

In the early stages of enacting swing changes, you will likely experience a slight downturn in your game. In order to achieve permanent improvement over the long haul, however, you must accept these setbacks and persevere through them. Otherwise, the only recourse is to allow these compensations to compound, which ultimately will keep your game at the same level or even make it worse. In the end, staying the course is the only viable option.

FACILITATING YOUR LEARNING

In order for you to learn anything new, particularly in golf, you need good information, visual references, solid coaching, and time to practice. This book has provided you with proven, research-based information you can implement into your game immediately. It is important that you reread the information carefully to make sure you fully understand the individual passages. We don't want you to waste your time beating balls in futility, working on the wrong thing due to misinterpreting the information we have presented.

Before you review the entire program, ask yourself which parts of

FIG. 10-3. Those who are serious about identifying their swing problems and tracking their progress, will invest in a video camera.

the presentation struck a special chord with you. Were the illustrations especially helpful? Was it the text that drove home the points most clearly? Or was it the drills that ingrained the true sense of what we were trying to communicate? People not only learn at different rates, they also learn best through varying modes of presentation.

It may be that you, like most people, are a visual learner who, having watched a top PGA Tour player in action, transfers that image effectively into your swing. If that is the case, pay special attention to the images of the Pro and try to imitate his positions and flow of movement from one stage of the swing to the next.

If you are technically oriented (though fewer people are), you may best relate to the written word. In this case, you will find the text describing the movements of the Pro the most enlightening.

Finally, you may (like the best athletes) best learn by feeling the movements. If so, your most valuable learning tool will be the drills. Whatever your best mode of learning, recognize it and try to get your information in this format whenever possible.

If you are serious about performing our suggested drills, you should acquire a teaching shaft, metronome, and weighted club. They constitute a minor investment that will provide solid benefits.

You also will find it helpful to acquire a video camera, film your performance during practice, and note your progress visually (fig. 10-3). No doubt what you feel you are doing can vary dramatically from what you actually are doing. The camera never lies.

To maximize your improvement we also recommend you enlist a qualified person to observe your swing. Since we are in the teaching business, we believe that an investment in lessons from a qualified PGA or LPGA teaching professional is one of the best choices you can make in your golfing career. If you can't afford professional instruction, enlist the help of a good friend. It is very difficult to maximize your full potential all alone. Having a coach or friend will keep you accountable, push you a little harder during practice, and help you develop or maintain good mechanics. Outside help is valuable in other ways. A friend, teacher, or acquaintance also serves as motivator, sounding board, competitor, and progress evaluator.

PRACTICE, PRACTICE

Finally, it is vital that you commit to a consistent practice regimen. This means setting aside quality time to spend on the practice tee. Time is a precious commodity and it is all too easy to make your game take a backseat to other obligations. But if you feel recreation is important, and golf is a major part of that phase of your life, then you probably can find a way to practice and play.

Understand it is not just the volume of time that is important, but how you use what time you have. Come to the range with a plan and some immediate objectives.

There will be serious physical effort involved in your commitment too. We have witnessed the practice routines of Tom Kite and Greg Norman, and take our word for it, their work ethic is as fierce as any person in any walk of life. They are shining examples of athletes who are disciplined, motivated, smart, and enthusiastic. When they show up to practice, they do so with a specific agenda in mind. We have noted that golf is a game, but at the same time we do not believe it is a foolhardy pursuit. Things worth doing are worth doing well, and that applies to your approach to golf.

For the average golfers, just to simply maintain their current level of play requires a minimum of from 30 minutes to 1 full hour of practice a week during the golfing season. To demonstrate noticeable improvement requires anywhere from 2 to 5 hours per week. To attain significant improvement demands a minimum of at least 6 hours per week. This is not meant to discourage you in any way, but that observation may give you a rough idea as to exactly how much time you should devote to your goal.

What, specifically, can you do to make your practice sessions productive? First, as part of the plan we have suggested, you need a detailed list of what you hope to accomplish when you arrive at the range. To that end, it is smart to keep a note pad in your golf bag so you can keep a log of your swing and play thoughts, problems you are experiencing, how your goals are progressing, and where you left off at the end of each practice session (fig. 10-4). Most dedicated PGA and LPGA pros do this. They warm up prior to their rounds then, as they play, take notes not only on the golf course but on how they are playing. When they arrive at the practice range after the round is over, their objectives are clear and they get right to work.

A word of caution. Many times golfers tend to practice the things they are doing well rather than the things that they are struggling with. That, or they merely blast driver shots as hard as they can, because they find that more exhilarating than hitting the 8-iron. Your practice sessions should be balanced with adequate attention devoted to the full swing, short game, trouble shots, and mental game. Work on your strengths, but keep in mind that the greatest improvement will come when you improve your weaknesses.

It is also important to spend some of your time practicing as you would if you were on the course. Harvey Penick used to ask Tom Kite to chip and putt with only one ball. He would

FIG. 10-4. Taking notes while playing allows you to identify your future practice goals. It also serves as a reminder that these problems need to be solved on the practice tee, not on the golf course.

tell Tom that since you only get one ball when you play, the same should hold true when you practice. That goes especially for your preshot routine. As you hit balls, make it a point to go through your full routine on every third ball you hit.

Always make a clean delineation between the practice range and the golf course. The wrong place to practice your swing is on the golf course, where you are thinking of ways to score, not thinking of swing mechanics. This is easier said than done. We all have been guilty of working on swing key number 25 by the eighth hole. But when you are playing the course, discipline yourself to keep your swing keys simple, not more than one or two at most. And avoid changing them during the round. Jack Nicklaus was once asked if he utilized swing thoughts when he was in position to win a big tournament, or if he just stepped up and hit the ball. Jack said he normally played with one or two swing keys during every round. He cited keys such as "transfer your weight to the right heel on the backswing and then transfer it to the left heel on the follow-through" as typical reminders.

FIG. 10-5. The full swing is only the first of many parts of the game that need to be carefully researched. Analysis of various aspects of the short game is only one of the exciting possibilities.

COME AND SEE US

Although it has taken us seventeen years to put this information together, it is far from our final effort. We will continue to learn from both our continued research and teaching efforts. We have so much more to discover in areas like the short game, trouble shots, and uneven lies, to name just a few (fig. 10-5). And what do the factors such as age, gender, strength, flexibility, and club selection have to do with the golf swing? All of these opportunities indicate that we have a long, exciting journey of discovery ahead.

If you want to keep up with our teaching and research efforts, visit us on the Internet at www.compusport.com. Technology is providing us with interesting new ways to communicate, and golf instruction will benefit tremendously.

FINALLY, GOOD LUCK

Our greatest hope is that you've enjoyed your first trip through *Swing Like a Pro.* If that is the case, it's a sure bet that even greater enjoyment lies in store. The greatest joy in golf lies in improving, and the findings of our research and proven methods of dispensing this information guarantees you will get better. We wish we could be there to see the results: the pride and feeling of accomplishment you will experience over the next few months, the astonished looks on your friends' faces as you strike the ball like never before, and the low numbers on your scorecard that your rivals will find hard to believe.

It's all yours for the taking. Congratulations in advance for a job well done.